The American Way

Additional Works
by Mark Fennell

Books:
The American Way
Making America Great
The Best You Can Get
Lonely Roads

Websites:
www.inspirationalwriting.info
www.eminutemen.com

Speaking Engagements:
Contact author to arrange public speaking engagements.
Special rates for community groups.
Contact: markpoet@aol.com

The American Way

Part of the Making America Great series

Mark Fennell

iUniverse, Inc.
New York Lincoln Shanghai

The American Way

iUniverse, Inc.

For information address:
iUniverse, Inc.
2021 Pine Lake Road, Suite 100
Lincoln, NE 68512
www.iuniverse.com

ISBN: 0-595-31038-9

Printed in the United States of America

Contents

The American Way: Preface ix

Part I   *Basics of the American Way* *1*

Basic Truths about America 3

The American Character 5

Limited Government. 7

The people control their lives and The people control the
    government 9

Part II   *Government and Freedoms.* *15*

Balance of Power. 17

The people check the government. 24

The Second Amendment exists in case the government ignores all
    the others 27

Freedom of Speech 38

Freedom of Religion 43

Freedom, Responsibility, and Ethics .53

Part III   *Religion in the United States* *55*

Founding Fathers Were Religious 57

Government and Religion: Self-government does not exclude God. . . .62

We are a church going people 66

Christmas in America—the Universal Holiday 71

Summary of Religion, Government, and America 73

Part IV   Economics and Success in America *77*

Free Market Economy and Running Your Own Business 79

Anyone can Succeed: Opportunity for All 92

Freedom, Choice, and Success 98

Government, Taxes, and Budgets 103

We do not steal to become successful 112

Part V   Being a Good American *121*

Melting Pot and Becoming a Good American 123

Good Neighbors and Community Spirit 129

Civics: duties in self-government 137

Patriotism 143

Un-American activities and dirty words 146

Part VI   Preserving and Protecting the American
           Way *151*

Rule of Law and Judicial System 153

The government is not above the people 163

Punishing bad behavior and illegal acts 168

Preserving the American Way at Home 174

Protecting America Abroad: Freedom Isn't Free 184

Ethics in America 189

Teaching the American Way: Courses in Civics and History. 193

Modern Issues and the American Way 203

Property Rights and abuses of Eminent Domain. 209

Improving America 216

Part VII Conclusion*. *223

Conclusion 225

APPENDIX A   Understanding America. 231

APPENDIX B   Civic groups and volunteer organizations. 233

APPENDIX C   Groups to join to help preserve the American
Way. 235

APPENDIX D   Suggested laws to ensure the American Way 241

The American Way: Preface

The old Superman comics spoke of "Truth, Justice, and the American Way." There is an "American Way." Unfortunately, too many people in this country no longer know what that means.

The term "American Way" used to mean something. However, over the last fifty years, people have torn away at America, trying to destroy our precious American Way. Unfortunately, to a large degree, they have been successful.

We who know better must return our nation to The American Way.

I wrote this book to explain the American Way. This is more than just a civics book or a collection of quotes, this is a book to teach the American Way.

I would like readers of all ages and backgrounds to understand America better. If you have been taught incorrectly before about America, then maybe this book will help open your eyes. If you are one of those who does understand America, then maybe you can use this book—in a classroom setting or given to people you know—to help teach those who don't understand.

<u>Teaching about the American Way</u>

Although writing about morals and the American tradition is not necessarily new, this has been weak in the past thirty years.

Since the founding of our country, teachers and writers of all types have been teaching the great ideas. The keys are there, they just need to be taught to new generations, and must be stated in new ways. Everyone who understands how great America is eventually comes to the conclusion that we must teach our children and teach immigrants about America so that the greatness of America continues.

Sadly, America is not teaching civics anymore. Most schools nationwide have dropped civics long ago. Nor does America teach proper history. History classes teach that America is a bad place, not a great one. Even if the class is favorable to America, much good history is neglected.

Immigrants also are a problem. In the past, we have been the great melting pot. For hundreds of years people from all nations and all religious backgrounds have come to this continent for a new and better life. Most of our history is one of immigrants really appreciating their freedoms, and making great successes for themselves.

Today this has changed. Too many immigrants today see America as a free give-away. They think that they can just come in, hold out their hand, and get riches. I know many cases of recent immigrants who broke law after law, and still they wanted more. They push for more government and business give-aways—and still they want more. They steal from America, and yet they insult America while they steal. There are even books printed in other countries which tell the people how to make the most of taking from the United States.

These recent immigrants must be taught the American Way. It is essential that we do so.

Socialists are a major threat

The socialists are a major threat. They push their way into the government. They create law after law, faster than we can work up the coalition to stop them. While most of us are busy living our lives, earning money, and just being good Americans, these socialists in government are busy at work destroying our country.

Being the webmaster for the e-minutemen, I get lots of news, most of which is not reported in the main media. The feeling I often get is a dam that is about to burst. The liberals keep drilling holes, and a few of us try to stop the hole. But there are so many of them, and so few of us who are aware of their vandalism, that it is all we can do to work at a frantic pace trying to keep the dam from bursting open.

That dam I speak of is the American Way. The liberal-socialists are working hard to tear it down. The American people don't want it down. The American people like it, but they don't often realize what damage the socialists are doing until it is too late.

<u>Overall goal of the book</u>

The overall goal for this book is this: I want you to have a better understanding of America, a greater appreciation of America, and be more willing to work to protect America.

I will be objective, but I will also be passionate. I will talk about civics, the Constitution, and history, but I will also talk of other issues which are of concern for our nation today.

Whoever you are who reads this, I want you to have a better understanding of The American Way. I want you to understand the many characteristics of America. I want you to understand the proper role of government. I want you to understand morals and religious freedoms. I want you to realize what the American culture is, and that it has been around, and working quite well, for over 200 years.

I want you to become an American, in the truest sense of the word. I want you to live as an American, to appreciate the many wonderful things that only America has. I want you to perpetuate the culture of America—by living it, by fighting for it, and by teaching it.

Be proud of The American Way.

M.F.

PART I

Basics of the American Way

Basic Truths about America

1. The Constitution exists to limit the government, not to limit the people.

The people retain their powers and protect their freedoms.

2. Our "Rights" come from God. Our Rights come from our natural existence. These rights do *not* come from government.

The Bill of Rights was created so that no man, no government, could take away the rights that naturally belong to us.

3. There is a distinct American culture.

We are a nation founded on ideals, a vision based upon morals.
We have a system of laws and justice, with checks and balances, and administered by the people.
Honesty, trust, courtesy, and compassion do matter, and these are integral parts of the American fabric.
We are the true Land of Brotherhood, because Americans know that we must have consideration, kindness, and positive relationships with our neighbors.

4. Out of Many, One

My ancestors may have come from a dozen nations, but I am 100% American.

5. Success in America depends on two things:
   a) The Freedoms we have unique to this country
   b) An individual's determination and personal sacrifice.

Success in America is *not* determined by a man's economics, his race, or by the government.

6. Freedom of speech exists for healthy dialogue and for personal expression.

However, Americans should restrain this freedom when it comes to speech that is hateful, insulting, or outright lies.

7. Freedom of Religion means Freedom to Be Religious.

This nation was founded by men who believed in God. As an American, I have the right to believe in God, to give thanks, and to celebrate Christmas.

As an American, I can respect your beliefs, but I do not have to change my religious practices or to stop being religious.

8. Our freedoms give us choice:

We can choose to stay or leave, to listen or ignore, to be active or passive. Americans are free to choose who we associate with, where we work, and how we live our lives.

How we choose to use these freedoms is up to us, yet so is the protection of those same freedoms.

The American Character

The American Character is a combination of ethics, independence, community spirit, civic duty, and religious convictions. The following is a list of the traits of the American Character.

Ethics
1. Honesty
2. Trust
3. Fairness
4. Integrity
5. Courtesy
6. Respect
7. Tolerance
8. Manners
9. Kindness

Independence
10. Self-reliant
11. Hard working
12. Risk taking
13. Exploring, creating, and innovating
14. Entrepreneurial—building his own business
15. Takes life's problems in stride, with wisdom and a smile
16. Laughs often—even in adversity and at himself
17. Dreamer with a can-do attitude

Community spirit
18. Law abiding
19. Belief in Equality—no class system, and equal treatment for all
20. Will not use freedom as excuse for unlimited behavior
21. Does not take advantage of others
22. Cares about his neighbor; is helpful and generous

Civic duty
23. Takes active part in his neighborhood
24. Loves his country
25. Appreciates America's Freedoms, and will defend them
26. Preserves and teaches the American culture
27. Stops unethical and un-American behaviors

Religious convictions
28. Devotion to God
29. Church going
30. Has faith—in God, in America, in himself, and in the future

Limited Government

Basic Truth of America #1. The Constitution exists to limit the government, not to limit the people. The people retain their powers and protect their freedoms

Limited government is one of the most essential pieces of the United States of America.

In an ideal world, the people would govern themselves totally, and there would not be a need for any laws. However, even in the best world, some government is always needed. Nevertheless, we must always remember that we should aim for that ideal goal of almost no government.

There are several dimensions to this concept:

1. Individuals run their own lives.
    Individuals are allowed to make their own choices, and to live their lives as they see fit, without the government telling people what they can and cannot do.

2. Behavior is persuaded, not legislated.
    Individuals choose to behave well and be ethical, because it is good for all. Businesses and communities police themselves. It is best to not legislate on behavioral issues if at all possible.

3. Local government serves the people best.
    The closer the government body is to the people, the better they understand the needs, and the better decisions will be made. City government, local school boards, local police and fire departments—these are the government organizations best able to meet the needs of the people.

4. Charity is run best by the community.

Americans are generous, and do like to help their neighbor. This is much more effective, and is more satisfying, if done at the local level.

Welfare, helping the poor and disabled, helping a neighbor through a job loss or tragedy, these are things better done by the local people themselves. The people will know who to help, and how to help them best. The money that people donate will be better used. It is also much better for maintaining that sense of community which is so important to everyone.

<u>Summary</u>

Limited government is a key element in the American Way. The people choose how to run their own lives, and the local government and local people know best how to help their own communities.

There are many people who wish to grow the government. This is absolutely wrong. This is not the American Way.

The people control their lives and The people control the government

A central element to the American Way is that the people are in control.

There are two important manifestations of this:

    1. The people control their own lives
    2. The people control the government

These elements are unique to America. These elements are distinct to our government and to our way of life. In other countries, the government dictates how the people can live. This is not so in America. Here in the United States, each person has full control over his own life, and the people as a whole run the government.

1. <u>The people control their own lives</u>

This is perhaps the most significant element to America. The American Way is for each person to have freedom to live his life as he wants.

<u>The Founding Documents guarantee individuals control their lives</u>

The founding documents of our nation ensure that the people control their own lives.

The Declaration of Independence states: "We hold these truths to be self-evident, that all men are created equal, that they are endowed by their Creator with certain unalienable Rights, that among these are Life, Liberty and the pursuit of Happiness."

The Constitution guarantees our Freedoms, specifically in the Bill of Rights. The First Amendment is perhaps the most significant to ensuring that the people control their own lives: "Congress shall make no law respecting an establishment of religion, or prohibiting the free exercise thereof; or abridging the freedom of speech, or of the press; or the right of the people peaceably to assemble, and to petition the Government for a redress of grievances."

The Fourth Amendment is also important in this area of personal freedom: "The right of the people to be secure in their persons, houses, papers, and effects, against unreasonable searches and seizures, shall not be violated, and no Warrants shall issue, but upon probable cause, supported by Oath or affirmation, and particularly describing the place to be searched, and the persons or things to be seized."

Finally, the Ninth and Tenth Amendments, the last two of the Bill of Rights, state specifically that the people retain their rights. The Ninth Amendment states: "The enumeration in the Constitution, of certain rights, shall not be construed to deny or disparage others retained by the people."

The Tenth Amendment states: "The powers not delegated to the United States by the Constitution, nor prohibited by it to the States, are reserved to the States respectively, or to the people."

The essence of these last two Amendments is this: We who wrote the Constitution probably couldn't think of every area that the government might try to take over from the people. However, even though we have not specifically stated everything, it is assumed that the people, not the Federal government, have most authority and freedom. In the great majority of areas, the people retain their rights.

America is great because people control their own lives

America works because everyone pursues their happiness. America works and is far more successful than any other nation precisely because the people are able to make the best choices for themselves.

We will discuss many specifics of how this works throughout this book. Here are but a few highlights.

Americans choose how to live their lives. They can choose lifestyles, careers, and personal pleasures. Because of these choices, each American is more likely to be happier than if he wasn't allowed these choices.

Free market economy benefits everyone. People are free to make and sell any goods they want. The people are free to buy any goods they want. The end results include: everyone gets products they want, competition makes products the best they can be, and innovation occurs more frequently.

Progress can occur more easily. Because the people can run their own lives, the American spirit has always been one of exploration and innovation. Because people are allowed free expression, then concepts are spread more quickly. Because of the free market economy, good technology and ideas will spread.

Just as important, all change in America is peaceful and evolutionary. We don't need a revolution like Communists believe—just our freedom to control our own lives.

Note that controlling your own life and pursuing your pleasures does not mean being selfish. In fact, Americans are very generous. Nor does this imply that we don't compromise. As communities, we have to compromise. Indeed, Americans are as community oriented as they are self-reliant. They are as ethical as they are free. This combination makes America successful and more satisfied than any other nation in the world.

The fact that Americans are allowed to live their own lives makes the best of everything. We will show this throughout the book.

2. <u>The people control the government</u>

The government is run by the people. This is distinct from many other nations in which the government is run by a dictator.

In America, the people choose representatives to run the government. These representatives are accountable to the people.

The only reason we have representatives is because it would be difficult for each person in America to both earn a living and to vote on every issue. Furthermore, because we have different areas to govern—city, state, and federal—it would be impossible for one person to be in all these legislatures at the same time. To prevent things from becoming cumbersome, we hire representatives. They represent us in the government affairs. They represent us only because we cannot realistically be there in person to discuss and vote on every issue.

Nevertheless, the representatives are supposed to truly be identical to us. They should vote as we would vote, if we were there. They should act as we would act. We choose a representative because we think his judgment on issues closely resembles our own.

It is very important to remember that those in government are responsible to us. We are not responsible to them. Remember, also, that we hired them. If they do not do the job we hired them for, then we fire them and get a replacement.

United States as a business

Those people we choose to represent us in government should be no different from those who represent us in business. Those people we hire to represent us in government should believe what we believe, speak the way we would speak, and act the way we would act.

When we run a business, we often hire people to do various jobs. These jobs may include manufacturing, advertising, sales, payroll, and accounting. Sometimes we hire these people because we do not want to do these jobs—we are not specialists, nor do we want to be. We also hire people for these jobs because our company is too large for just one person to do all of it himself.

So it is with the government. We need the jobs done, but it would be impractical for the people to be involved in all the jobs that need doing. We hire people to do the jobs for us.

The primary government employees we call representatives. These representatives act as our agents. We give them legal authority, often called proxy, to make judgments on our behalf when it is not practical for us to be there in person.

Because there are many levels of government, we hire many representatives: city council and mayor, state legislature and governor, U.S. Congress and President. There are several different jurisdictions, and so we must hire an employee to represent us for each area. Nevertheless, each representative is an employee working for us, the people.

The secondary government employees are those in the various agencies and departments. The people in the various agencies and departments work for us as well. Every government employee is an employee of the people.

We must also remember that the people, as the managers of the government, are also the ones with the finances. The people create the income, then they share some of their money for the public good—hiring government employees and funding the community services. We must always remember that the money in the public treasuries belongs to the people, and that every government employee works for the people.

Communicating with our representatives

The representatives must communicate with us, and they must also be open. These elements of the job are too often overlooked.

Those we hire for the government must communicate with us regularly so that we know what their intentions are. Similarly, it is our obligation to communicate with our representatives regularly. We must do this so that the representatives know what we, their bosses, expect from them on certain issues.

For example, in the business world we might hire a lawyer to negotiate a contract. As another example, we may hire a public spokesman to speak to the press on our behalf. These people we hire must truly represent us. The lawyer must not discuss terms that we are not willing to abide by. The public spokesman must not say things about our company we disapprove of.

Thus, in this business example, even though these people represent us, even though we have given them authority in certain areas, these people we hired must do as we say. Furthermore, these people we hire must communicate with us regularly, so that we know what their intentions are.

In the business world, managers have meetings all the time. For some managers, it is a daily morning meeting. For other managers it is a quarterly report and discussion. Regardless of the schedule, all good managers meet with their employees, or get memos from their employees, on some regular schedule so that the managers and the employees are consistent.

Government does not do this enough. In many cases, the government does not do this at all. The government must communicate regularly to the people. Suggestions on effective two-way communication with all areas of government can be found in the Appendix.

Being open is also important. Our representatives cannot keep secrets from us for we are their bosses.

We must know how they voted on every bill. We must know their position on every issue that comes up. We must know how they spend our money. Each of our representatives must be absolutely accountable. We have the right to ask any questions regarding their job, and they must answer us truthfully.

Note that the only exception to this full disclosure would be the area of national security.

This is just good business, and this makes good government as well. We are the bosses, the representatives are our employees. We need to understand this relationship and communicate continuously in both directions in order to ensure that we have best government.

Again, Suggestions on effective two-way communication with all areas of government can be found in the Appendix.

PART II

Government and Freedoms

Balance of Power

Introduction

The Founding Fathers wrote the Constitution so that the government would have a balance of power. They knew that it was important that no single man, nor any group of people, have too much power over the people.

The basic division they came up with was a system of 3 branches: legislative, executive, and judicial. In addition, there are other checks on government power such as free speech, free press, and all the rights of the people. All of these will be discussed throughout the book.

In the most basic understanding: The Legislative branch makes the laws. The Executive branch executes the laws. The Judicial branch interprets the laws.

Basic understanding: Legislature

The legislative branch consists of our representatives. We elect them to represent us at the capitol, and they will discuss public business on our behalf. They write the laws. They are the only branch of government authorized to do so.

The legislature is restricted in power because we elect all members of the legislature. The legislature is further given balance by being two bodies. The House of Representatives is apportioned by population. Each member represents the same number of citizens as every other member. The other body is Senate, which is given two Senators per state, regardless of state size. This creation of two bodies was done to make sure that larger or more populous states would not automatically have more power than the rest of the country.

It is important to again note these things: 1) The people elect the legislature, 2) the legislature is the only body that has authority to make the laws.

Basic understanding: Executive

The executive branch executes the laws. For example, the President appoints people to various positions in the government, in order to do the jobs of the public good. The President also represents America in foreign affairs.

Yet the President has many other jobs. The President sets the tone for the times, he has the vision, and he leads the people and the Congress to do great things. Note that this quality of leadership is very important, for any executive branch in our country—mayor, governor, or president.

To ensure a balance of power, the President's powers are limited and checked. Even Alexis de Tocqueville noted this, in his classic book "Democracy in America." De Tocqueville noted how "weak" the President's powers are, particularly when contrasted with the executive branch in his own country, the King of France.

There are good reasons for this. The Founders of the United States did not want a king, and they were very concerned about an executive with too much power. The founders knew that even an elected executive could become tyrannical and oppressive if his powers weren't limited to begin with.

Here are but a few examples where the President's powers are limited.

1) The President does not pass laws. The President proposes legislation, but only Congress can actually pass the laws. This was done so that many representatives create the laws, not just one man.

2) The Congress holds the finances. Congress, not the President, has authority over taxes and spending. The President certainly leads in these areas: he proposes budgets, asks for reduction in taxes, and encourages Congress to limit spending. However, only Congress, not the President, has Constitutional authority over the finances. This was done so that many representatives control the finances, not just one man.

A few more examples: 3) The President cannot declare war or ratify treaties without Congress. 4) The President is elected by the people. 5) The President serves a term of office, rather than serving for life.

These are but a few examples. It is in this way that no President can become too powerful over the people.

However, that is not to say the President is totally weak. The President's real power lies in his leadership.

As with all executive positions in this nation, the President must be a leader. The President sets the tone, he has the vision, and he takes the country in directions that are good for us. He explains to the people what he wants to do, and convinces the people that it is the right thing for the nation. He persuades members of both houses of Congress to pass his bills and support his proposals. This leadership is where an executive has real influence.

Here are but a few examples of significant Presidential leadership from our history. From 1800–1900: Thomas Jefferson sent Lewis and Clark on their scientific expedition, and then doubled our nation's size—peacefully—through the Louisiana Purchase. Abraham Lincoln led the nation through the civil war, keeping our nation together and ending slavery in this country forever.

From 1900–2000: Theodore Roosevelt increased the land in our National Parks, and he built the Panama Canal. John F. Kennedy started the Peace Corps, he persuaded Americans to do more for their country, and he led Americans to be the first people to land a man on the moon. Ronald Reagan revived our economy, won the Cold War, and brought freedom to many nations around the world.

In 2001: George W. Bush comforted the people when we were attacked, and he resolved to fight terrorism wherever we may find it

These are but a few examples of Presidential leadership.

To sum up the executive branch: the Founders of this nation limited the President's Constitutional authority in order to prevent any President from becoming too powerful. In spite of this, the position of President is a strong position, for he is in fact the elected leader of the government. He is the human face of the complex national government, and he is our representative to the world.

We should also remember that for any executive position in America—mayor, governor, or president—the situation is similar. The greatest real powers of any executive reside not as much in his Constitutional authorities as in his character, his vision, and his leadership.

Basic understanding: Judicial

The Judicial branch is of the most concern today. It is this branch which is misunderstood. It is this branch which has been grossly overstepping its bounds, and acting in a contrary way to the Constitution.

Therefore, the most important topic for discussion in this chapter is the Judicial branch.

The role of the judicial branch is to interpret laws. The judges look at the existing laws, and apply them to each case. That is their only role.

Judges overstepping their authority—what they cannot do

Judges cannot write law. Judges are not given that role in the Constitution. A judge who tries to change the law is overstepping his legal authority.

Judges cannot ignore the law. It doesn't matter whether a judge agrees with the law or not, all judges must follow the laws as they exist.

Note that each American sees at least one law that he doesn't agree with. However, that doesn't give us the right to just ignore the laws we don't like. We would be put in jail.

The reason for this is that the rule of law goes both ways. We will discuss rule of law in another chapter. Here note that if an American wants to be treated equally under the law, then that American must also act equally in following the law to begin with.

The same holds true for judges. Judges must follow the law and they must uphold the law. They cannot ignore the law.

<u>Judges cannot go against the will of the people</u>. The judge is but one person. Even a higher court is but a few individuals. Who are they to decide for the will of *millions* of people? They cannot.

We will discuss in this book that American communities and American government are run by the will of the people. What the people in a community want, they get to have. No judge is allowed to say otherwise. This includes all levels of community jurisdictions—city, state, and federal.

Any judge that goes against the will of the people is not fit to be judge. By definition, a judge who goes against the will of the people is not qualified to make judgments on their behalf.

<u>Judges cannot go against the American Way</u>. There is an American Way. Any judge who rules in contrast to any part of the American Way is not fighting for America, he is fighting against America. These men are not qualified to be judges.

<u>No judge can reject a law voted on by the people</u>. When the people vote directly for a law through a state ballot, no judge has the right to overturn the law.

I realize that some scholars will state that one role of the judicial branch is to overturn any laws that are un-Constitutional. This is good in theory, but not in practice.

The first flaw in the way judges "consider" the laws is this: many of the laws that the judges reject are not in any way in conflict with either the state constitution, nor in conflict with the US Constitution. Therefore, the judges are throwing out perfectly legitimate laws.

Second, these judges *themselves* are in conflict with the Constitution. If anything, we should throw out those judges, not the laws. These judges ignore laws they don't like, they rewrite laws, and they overturn good laws. All these actions are in direct conflict with the Constitution. These judges, not the laws, are un-Constitutional. The judges, not the laws, need to be thrown out.

Judicial reform: proposed laws

We have a very serious problem in America, one which puts our way of life in danger. That problem is the rise of un-American, un-Constitutional, activist judges.

Whenever a new problem comes along in government abuses, new laws must often be created to address these abuses. So it is now.

Here are a few suggested laws that each state government and the Federal government should enact regarding judicial reform. These have been collected from a variety of sources who discuss this subject.

Note that this is but a brief list. A fuller list may be found in the Appendix.

1. All judges must be elected directly by the people. They will not be appointed by legislatures. This includes state supreme court judges, federal circuit court judges, and the U.S. Supreme Court judges.

2. All judges, including state supreme court judges and federal circuit judges, must be re-elected every few years. No judge will serve for life.

3. Any law voted for directly by the people must be put into effect. No state court or Federal Circuit court can stall the law or legally prohibit it. Only the U.S. Supreme Court will be allowed to consider if the law is Constitutional. This provision must be stated specifically as law in each state's legal code as well as federal law.

4. Any judge, including state supreme court judges and federal circuit judges, can be recalled by the people. Recalling may be done if the judge oversteps his legal authority, if the judge rules in a way contrary to the will of the people, or if the judge rules contrary to the American Way.

5. All states should have an easy method for referendums. This means that the people are able to propose laws and then vote on them directly on a ballot.

6. All issues of religion and government should be voted on directly by the people. These issues include: public display of the Ten Commandments, saying prayer at public functions, and keeping God in the Pledge. On such important

issues, the people of the community must decide directly, and not let it be handled by a few judges.

Summary

The United States has a nice system of balance of power. The Constitution allows for checks and balances, in many areas, so that no one person, nor any one body, has too much power.

Unfortunately, today the Judicial branch is becoming an oligarchy. They want to write laws, ignore laws, and go against the will of the people. The rulings by judges at all levels have taken America down a terribly dangerous path. Activist judges could mean our destruction if we do not stop them.

The Constitution was wisely written to prevent such abuses of power. The judges are clearly going against the Constitution. Thus, there is no problem there—the judges are overstepping their authority, so they must be fired.

The difficulty lies in how judges get their jobs—appointed by legislatures, and often holding a position for life. We can change this. We elect our representatives; therefore we should elect our judges. We can recall representatives, so we should be able to recall judges. Representatives must re-apply every few years, so that no one can serve for life after just one election. Therefore, no judge should serve for life either.

Thus, the principles are there. The Constitution is clear. We merely need to get new, specific laws passed which will address this serious problem and make all judges more accountable to the people.

The people check the government

The Checks and Balances that we talk of usually reference the three branches of government. However, another outside source is just as important in checking the powers of the government: The People.

There several ways the people check the government.

<u>Elections</u>

All people who want the position of representing us must apply for the job. We look at their qualifications, and elect the one we think best.

Our representatives must reapply for their job every few years. They must convince us why they are the still the best for the job. We renew their term, or replace them if they are not satisfactory, through the process of elections.

<u>Freedom of Speech, Freedom of Press</u>

Freedom of Speech is an important way in which the people check on the government.

Remember that we said that good government comes from communication, and that this communication must go both ways. Our representatives must communicate with us, and we must communicate with them. Our freedom of speech allows for serious dialogue between the people and their representatives.

Furthermore, the people often must be critical of the government. I do not mean this in a negative way at all. No, what I mean is that the representatives work for us, and they are legislating on complex issues. Therefore, we must make certain we agree with their solutions to problems. We must be sure that our representatives share our judgment on most issues.

It is for these reasons that we must be critical of the government, in an altruistic and objective sense. We must be allowed to know everything the government does, and be able to discuss whether we think these actions are the best for our communities.

Therefore, a Free Press and our Freedom of Speech are essential tools for ensuring that our government is the best for the people. This ensures that the government's power stays limited, this ensures that those in the government behave ethically, and this ensures that those in government truly represent the people.

<u>Putting laws on the ballot</u>

In many states and communities, the constitution allows the people to propose a law, which is then put on the ballot for the people to vote on. This is democracy in its purest form.

Thus, if the representatives continue to fail in doing what the people want, then the people can do it for themselves. The law gets proposed, the people vote, and the law gets put into place—all done in spite of the representatives who failed in their jobs of representing the people.

It is very important to note that if the people pass a law in this way, then that law must stand. It can NOT be overturned by any court. The entire premise of our government is democracy: the people choose what they want for their communities. Once the people have spoken on a law in this way, then no court has a right to stand in the way of what the people want.

<u>Summary</u>

In America the people run the government. Thus, the people are allowed many ways to check on the government.

The people who work in the government work for us, and we get to hire or replace them through elections. Free speech is important to have dialogue with our representatives, and free press is important to expose those in government who overstep their bounds.

The people make the laws. Usually this is done through representatives, which the people choose. However, the people themselves may also put laws up for a vote, and these will be voted on by the people. Hence, if the legislature is not doing the will of the people, then the people have an alternate route to get their work done.

The Second Amendment exists in case the government ignores all the others

The most important reasons for the Right to own guns are:

1) To make sure that Americans are free and that our Rights are not taken away.

This is not just from foreign threats, but more importantly from those here in this country who try to create a dictatorship.

2) To protect your home, your property, your money, and your personal safety when criminals strike.

Wherever there is something of value, a criminal will try to take it. Often, these criminals have guns, so then should we. We must be allowed to protect ourselves and our property.

1) <u>Owning guns to keep America Free.</u>

This is the main reason for guns.

Why do you think the Founders thought this important enough to put as a Right in the Bill of Rights? And why was it important enough to be number 2? Those questions alone should make you think about the seriousness of what the founders were doing, and of the importance of our Right to own guns.

The government comes from the people. If leaders of the government ever try to control the people too much, then we must stop them. Normally this will happen through checks and balances, through free press, and through voting. However, should a few people ever get really serious, and start turning this country into a dictatorship, the people will stop them—with force.

These dictator leaders would love for us not to own weapons. They would have guns. We wouldn't. We wouldn't be able to fight back. Our free America would fall into a dictator's empire. There are plenty of studies which verify this—choose a dictator, choose a fascist country or communist country—this point is easily demonstrated.

We don't have to use these guns often, just knowing we can is a deterrent. An example: many police will tell you that they rarely fire their gun on the street. Just having the gun is a deterrent. In the worst cases, it is used when necessary. However, it does not need to be fired that much.

So it is with our Freedoms. Those evil leaders who want to have power, who take our liberties away, and who lie to the public…they would have no qualms about turning the government into a full dictatorship. The only thing holding them back is the 2nd Amendment. The only thing preventing America from becoming a dictatorship is our Right as Americans to own guns.

The very existence of the Second Amendment prevents many would-be dictators from taking that final step and oppressing the people.

Communist countries should be a warning to us

I spent some time in East Germany and East Berlin several years ago. The image remains clear. It is the warning I see for us if our right to own guns is taken away.

Keep in mind that when I was there Communism was in full power, and a real threat.

To understand the reason for the differences you must know the history of World War Two. I know that many people do not know their history, so I must briefly explain a few things. In essence, the Soviets took control of the eastern area of Germany. America and the western allies took control over the western area of Germany.

To further complicate issues was Berlin. Berlin was technically in East Germany, but was divided into two parts. The western allies joined their parts together, but the Soviets did not give up their piece.

America is not an imperialistic country. America is a liberating country. Therefore, the Americans brought democracy to the area, they brought the free market, and then they left the people alone to govern themselves.

In contrast, the Soviets kept a much tighter influence over their territories. That is why the eastern area was known as the "Soviet Block" even though there were technically different countries.

In some ways, this made a clear experiment. Different areas using each of the two methods for decades were enough to see the results. I spent time in both areas. The following is what I saw in East Germany and East Berlin—that is, the areas where the Communists had taken control.

In East Germany (Communist rule), military was everywhere. There were soldiers on the trains. There were soldiers in the public square. There were also tanks and other military vehicles traveling around. Note that these are not friendly sorts of military. No, the soldiers I saw in Eastern Europe looked seriously menacing. They weren't kidding around. In contrast, I've seen the US military, and military of other western nations, and they were usually friendly. This was not the case with the military I saw in East Germany. I have never seen a sight like this, in all my travels, before or since.

East Berlin had its own issues. The Communists built the Berlin Wall, which was an ominous structure. The communists built this thing across the entire length of the city, in order to prevent their own people from leaving. This wall was twice as high as any man, and made of solid concrete. The Communists topped this wall with barbed wire. No citizen would get out of the city without approval from the guards.

In contrast to East Berlin was West Berlin. In West Berlin, the people thrived. It was a regular city, with business and bustle. Yet over in East Berlin there was nothing—just empty streets. The only sign of life was the soldiers. The business centers of each part of Berlin were just a few miles apart in distance, but they were a thousand years apart in culture.

The train rides are long ones, with lots of time to think. Unlike rides on trains in Western Europe, no one talked on these East German trains. With soldiers on the train, and watching military vehicles go by outside, it feels more like you are being taken to the Gulag than that you boarded the train of your own free will.

I was glad to be out of there. Note that as a Westerner, I could leave. Many residents didn't have that option. I never took that for granted.

There is a common expression among those who support the Second Amendment: Gun control is not about guns, it is about control. This is so true. As I said earlier, the government would love for us to not have guns, for then they would be able to control us.

There are some Americans who want to take away our right to own guns. I know what such a world looks like. It looks like East Germany and East Berlin: Soldiers on trains. Walls with checkpoints. A dying city and a dying country. Keeping us inside our homes and inside our borders. We would not be allowed to really be free, and there would be no chance for prosperity or happiness.

I did not get this image from a book or from a movie. I saw it. It was real.

If you need a second image, just as real, look at the events at Tiananmen Square. Look upon that image of the lone man facing the tank. I understood the reality of that picture. I understood the tyranny, the bravery, and the fight for freedom regardless of personal cost.

There are many others who have seen this reality, in many countries. Anyone who has seen this tyranny inevitably becomes passionate about fighting for his freedoms. We must not take our freedoms for granted, and we must never let such oppression come to America. Our Right to own guns is essential to preventing such oppression.

The Communist control of East Europe has collapsed, and that is good. But it took a long, long time—precisely because the government controlled the people. It is difficult to be free when soldiers with guns rule the public areas.

Let us take lessons from history. Let us preserve our right to own guns, and thereby not let the United States to become like the dark days of Eastern Europe or see events such as at Tiananmen Square.

Need for our Right to own guns proven in 2000

The need for guns was most evident during the election of 2000, as Al Gore tried to steal the election.

There are many books, articles, and studies published regarding the election—even some done by those who wanted Al Gore to win. Any method used to count the votes show factually that George Bush won the election and that Al Gore lost. In addition, objective studies have uncovered a few illegal voting methods; all these illegal methods were a false count in favor of Gore.

Yet all Americans saw how Gore fought, using questionable counting methods, having Florida judges break the law to favor him. Let us not also forget a few illegal fundraising activities earlier on, and being caught in some outrageous lies about his life.

This man wanted to be President, and no law or ethical standard would get in his way. That is the sign of a dictator. That is a very dangerous sign. This man should never be an elected leader again.

Had Al Gore stolen the election and become President, millions of Americans would have taken arms to prevent his dictatorship. I, too, would have taken up arms and joined them.

I don't even own a gun. I've never fired a gun. Yet I love America and I love Freedom so much, that I would buy lots of guns, and join the millions of Americans who love America too. We would go into the street, march to Washington, and force Al Gore to be removed from the White House. We would force him to leave using guns. Thanks, Al, for proving the point so well.

Replacing oppressive leaders in government

This brings a similar point. Overthrowing the government is difficult, and it should be. However, if the people want it (as they would if a dictator stole the Presidency), then the people will rule. The government can hold back a few radicals, even a few hundred thousand spread throughout the country. However, the nation could never stop 200 million Americans, each armed and ready to fight for our beloved freedoms.

Thomas Jefferson made a similar point. "Prudence, indeed, will dictate that Governments long established should not be changed for light and transient causes; and accordingly all experience hath shewn, that mankind are more disposed to suffer, while evils are sufferable, than to right themselves by abolishing the forms to which they are accustomed. But when a long train of abuses and usurpations, pursuing invariably the same Object evinces a design to reduce them under absolute Despotism, it is their right, it is their duty, to throw off such Government, and to provide new guards for their future security."

Note that our Founding Fathers wisely created a system where oppressive government is less likely to happen than in other nations. Just as important, our Founding Fathers created a system where change in government can take place without bloody revolution.

We achieve these items through means such as: elections by the people; terms of office rather than serving for life; balance of power; free speech; and even through means such as impeachments and recalls. Thus, while other nations must go through revolutions in order to replace a tyrannical government, this is not so in America. Our Constitution allows the people to replace oppressive leaders in many ways without using violence.

However, just because we have a great system in America does not mean that we can be naive. There may come a time when the government oppresses the people. If there comes a time when the government thwarts the will of the people, when elections are frauds, and when the government uses force against the people, then we must be wary. We hope that such a time never comes. However, if it does, the people will be able to take back our government. The Second Amendment was put in place for just that contingency.

Always remember that we must fight while we can. After the dictators take control, as they did in Eastern Europe and in China, then it is too late. It much harder to fight for our freedoms later. That is the primary reason why the right to own guns is a fundamental right, and why it is #2 in the Bill of Rights.

To repeat: The Second Amendment exists primarily to prevent any potential dictator from taking full control over the people.

2) <u>To protect your home, your property, your money, and your safety when criminals strike.</u>

Wherever there is something of value, there will be a criminal trying to take it. We have a right to protect our property, and ourselves, at all times.

Often these criminals have guns, so then should we. Suppose that a man comes to your store with a gun. If you have a gun, then you can stop him. Suppose that a man holds a gun to you on the street. If you have a gun, then you can keep your money.

Furthermore, studies have shown that violent crimes are most quickly stopped if there is a "good gun." This means that a law-abiding American has a gun in his possession, and uses this gun to stop the violence in progress.

Here is a piece sent to me by a fellow activist American, concerned for Second Amendment Rights:

"Scientists studying school shootings have found that the single most important factor in preventing injury and death after a school shooting starts is how fast a "good gun" gets to the scene to stop the attack."

"In one attack a teacher saved many lives when he ran to his car, retrieved his licensed firearm, and then held the shooter for police. In another incident, an armed security guard was able to instantly pin down a shooter, saving countless children. A sad counterpoint to this is Columbine High School, where the SWAT team took 45 minutes to even enter the building. 15 children died and 27 were wounded."

"Until we as a nation can solve the alienation and anger that create these horrors, we must take all the practical steps we can to protect and defend our children if the unthinkable happens. 33 states have concealed carry laws. FBI statistics show violent crime has gone DOWN in those states."

"One criminologist, John Lott, even wrote a book about this, called "More Guns, Less Crime". His studies of these states have also shown that people with CHL licenses actually misuse their firearms less than the police!"

"Everyone who is issued a license must first pass a rigorous background check and safety testing. If the unimaginable happens, events have proven that Concealed Handgun Licensed citizens have an important advantage, for the lives saved will be measured in the seconds and minutes it takes for an armed citizen to get to the scene, whether it's a police officer, security guard or a civilian with a CHL permit."

Thus, states which allow concealed handguns actually have a decrease in crime. Citizens who carry these guns must pass a rigorous background check, as well as safety testing. Finally, these armed, law-abiding citizens save lives by being the first "good gun" to arrive on the scene after a violent criminal strikes.

To repeat: the Right to gun ownership is essential for the safety of all Americans.

Gun safety—the other side of the Second Amendment issue

The other side of the gun issue is on safety. I can understand this, and I will explain why. Yet, I emphasize up front that the Second Amendment is very important and we must preserve it.

I can understand the issue over gun safety. I will offer some personal examples.

1. A relative of mine was killed with a gun. It was a classic case of thinking the gun was not loaded. It was a tragic accidental death, and he died a teenager.
2. When I was teaching in one inner city school, the older brother of one of my students was shot in a gang related action.

3. I taught school during the time of the Columbine tragedy. All teachers and students were keenly aware for years of the potential.

4. As a teacher, I have seen violent students. They will use anything as weapons, therefore I know that the more we can keep guns away from these youth, the better all of us will be.

5. I was in Virginia during the time of the sniper shootings. I was in the cities, on the same nights, as the victims. The snipers shot 14 people in all before being caught. Each day I knew I could easily be the next victim.

So, you see, I understand fully the reasoning by Americans who are concerned with gun safety. Guns are indeed dangerous.

However, most gun owners are safe. Most gun owners are well trained in the proper use of guns, and they know how to be safe. Most gun owners have an intelligent respect for guns, they lock their guns away when not at home, and they teach their children gun safety. In many states, in order to carry a concealed gun you must be trained and certified. Sometimes the gun owners must be tested annually. Gun owners already go through detailed background checks. Those who fail the check are not sold guns.

It is criminals who abuse guns, not most Americans. The criminals are the ones who commit violent crimes. Criminals are the ones who shoot innocent people. Most of the time, these guns are gotten illegally, because background checks prevented these criminals from buying a gun legally in the marketplace.

As for accidental deaths and kids getting hold of guns, most adult gun owners are actually very responsible. Most parents prevent their kids from having access to guns. I know many gun owners who lock their guns away when not at home. For those parents who want protection by their bed, these owners simply have a routine: they unlock the gun and keep it close each night; then they lock it up again as a routine each morning. They also teach their kids to be respectful of the gun. These parents punish their children swiftly and severely if the children play with the gun.

Although accidental deaths and school shootings are tragic, these are not the norm. Most gun owning parents are very responsible. Most kids of gun owning parents are very responsible.

A refresher course for free citizens.

These are short statements which really clarify the issue. These were passed along to me by people who fight to protect the Second Amendment.

a. Free men do not ask permission to bear arms.
b. The Second Amendment is in place in case they ignore the others.
c. 64,999,987 firearms owners killed *no one* yesterday
d. The United States Constitution (c) 1791. All Rights reserved.
e. What part of "shall not be infringed" do you not understand?
f. If guns are outlawed, can we use swords?
g. If guns cause crime, then pencils cause misspelled words.
h. You don't shoot to kill; you shoot to stay alive.
i. Criminals love gun control—it makes their jobs safer.
j. Assault is a behavior, not a device.
k. If guns cause crime, then matches cause arson.
l. If you don't know your rights you don't have any.
m. Those who trade liberty for security have neither.
n. You only have the rights you are willing to fight for.
o. Enforce the "gun control laws" we have, don't make more.
p. Gun control is not about guns; it's about control.
q. Only a government that is afraid of its citizens tries to control them.
r. When you remove the people's right to bear arms, you create slaves.
s. The American Revolution would never have happened with gun control.
t. "…a government of the people, by the people, for the people…"

Summary

The Second Amendment is essential to preserving America's Freedoms. The Second Amendment is essential to letting Americans protect themselves from criminals. We must continually preserve the American Right to own guns.

Although there are real issues of guns and safety, we must *not* be extreme about controlling guns. We can have gun safety while keeping the Second Amendment. A full discussion would be a book in itself—and there are several books already in print. This is a discussion worth having; however we must agree at the beginning to preserve our Right to gun ownership.

It is much easier to prevent tyranny than it is to overthrow tyranny after we have become oppressed. The Second Amendment is essential to preventing such tyranny.

Freedom of Speech

Basic Truth #6
Freedom of speech exists for healthy dialogue and for personal expression. However, Americans should restrain this freedom when it comes to speech that is hateful, insulting, or outright lies.

Introduction

Freedom of Speech is one of our greatest freedoms. Too few nations have this freedom, and their society suffers.

Perhaps the most important reason for Free Speech to exist is so that the people can make sure the government does not get too powerful.

Dictators love to control the press. A dictator does not want any investigation into what he does. A dictator wants to control freedom of speech and the press in order to have control over the people. He wants to control information so that no one knows the truth—about the abuses of government, about the world around them, or even about their own country.

A press that is controlled, and speech that is limited, always makes the most oppressive of governments.

This is the primary reason for free speech. There are, however, many other benefits. There are also practical limitations. In this chapter we will look at a few of these.

Benefits of Freedom of Speech

We are a nation of self-government. That means the people themselves run the government. However, in order to run the government the best we can, we must have an open discussion of ideas. Therefore, we must have complete freedom of speech in order to have the most effective government.

Self-government also means that individuals run their own lives. However, to live your life well, it is best to be informed. Freedom of speech allows Americans to learn about a variety of topics, and to ask a variety of questions. Americans can research and experiment on any topic, then share their findings to their fellow Americans. It is in this way that every American can live a better life. We must have freedom of speech and freedom of press so that all individuals may be informed on any topic, and thus live their lives better.

Free speech also allows our society to change for the better. Just as important, free speech allows this progress to occur in peaceful ways. Americans can use their freedom of speech to persuade other Americans to agree on the issue. Americans can persuade other Americans to act in a certain way. Freedom of speech is essential for this to happen. Note that we do not need violence or revolution to make these changes, just our freedom of speech.

Freedom of speech and a free press is also very important to spread information about those bad people who wish to destroy America. As webmaster for the eminutemen, I get information on many, many things that the socialists are trying to do to this country. Most of these items are not reported in the main press. If it weren't for a few good internet news sources, and the readership of many members of our group, I would not hear of these un-American activities.

Even most people reading this page probably have little idea just how much the socialists are trying to destroy our country. That is because the socialist press has been effective. However, because this is still just business controlled, not government controlled, then many other smaller journalism companies (including internet, magazines, books, and radio) have the freedom to print the truth.

Because of our Freedom of Speech, several things happen: 1) good reporters can find this information and print it; 2) people can read about it; 3) readers can pass on this information, and 4) Americans can actively fight for our way of life.

Freedom of speech is also good for expression. It is healthy to express your mood and your feelings. Artists of all mediums, whether professional or hobbyists, need to create their art. Many other Americans want to enjoy that art.

As an artist and art-lover myself, I understand this. Thus, freedom of speech allows everyone to create and share their art and express their views without any interference from the government.

Practical limitations on Free Speech

"If you abuse the First Amendment, you will destroy it."

—Michael Landon

Freedom of Speech does have its limits. This was well understood from the earliest days. However, there are Americans who try to abuse this freedom.

Note that the element of people who abuse freedom of speech is nothing new. Throughout the history of America there have been people who lied and slandered. This was not limited to any profession—including people in the press, in politics, and in business. However, those who have abused freedom of speech have always been in the minority, for it is not the American Way. Like crime, this is just a problem that will never entirely go away. It is a problem we have to work hard to minimize on a regular basis.

Lying and slander are the main limits to free speech. You cannot lie about issues. You cannot make up facts just to suit your purpose. You cannot twist the truth, or alter the reality in your reporting. You cannot stage an event and pass it off as real. You cannot tell lies about another person. You cannot slander the name of a good American.

Lying about a person is wrong because it hurts his reputation. Lying about issues is wrong because when our facts are not accurate, then our discussions are flawed, which means that our solutions will not be any good.

Americans are sometimes limited in where they can speak. For example, you cannot shout criticisms while someone is giving a speech. You cannot disrupt private gatherings or destroy property.

Artists are also limited in their free expression. Free market usually dictates artistic expression. If the people find a particular piece of art too offensive, then the people don't buy it. The people also have the right to persuade the distributors and sponsors to remove it. Further, the people can state limits on where certain art can be shown, particularly that of a sexual nature or with excessive violence.

Censorship

The government cannot censor anyone. The First Amendment guarantees that.

However, people should censor themselves. In discussions, it is good manners to be polite and to stick with the issue. Under no circumstances should you become emotional, threatening, or insulting.

Artists should also censor themselves, for what I call "good taste." Artists should censor themselves for such items as violence, sex, and profanity.

For more detail on these topics, see my website at: www.inspirationalwriting.info

Summary

Our Freedom of Speech is one of our most important freedoms. It should not be taken lightly.

The most important reason to have free speech is to keep our government in check. Dictators around the world have stopped free speech and have controlled the press. This only leads to propaganda and to oppression of the people.

Even today, socialists are working hard to destroy our country and to oppress the people. Few people know what these enemies are doing, for they are doing many of these of these bad things in secret. Only through a free press and our freedom of speech can these atrocities be exposed, shared with the people, and then stopped.

We must also have free speech to have healthy dialogue. In that way we are able to run the government in the best manner.

However there are limits on free speech. You cannot lie. This means you cannot lie about facts on any issue, and you cannot slander a good person's name. You also cannot be disruptive or violent.

Thus, Freedom of Speech is essential to a free society. However, there are limits to this freedom. These limits are based on simple ethics: honesty, courtesy, and manners.

Freedom of Religion

Basic Truth of America #7:

Freedom of Religion means Freedom to Be Religious

This nation was founded by men who believed in God. As an American, I have the right to believe in God, to give thanks, and to celebrate Christmas.

As an American, I can respect your beliefs, but I do not have to change my religious practices or to stop being religious.

Founding Fathers were religious

America was founded by religious people. Many who came to America came here precisely for religious freedom. That means that they wanted to practice their religion as they wanted to without being stopped by the government.

The Founding Fathers were also religious. Jefferson refers to "Creator" in the Declaration of Independence. Washington was the first to declare Thanksgiving as an American Celebration. If you look at letters and speeches of the time, you will see that most people spoke of God as an accepted fact. These are but a few examples.

America was founded on religion. There is no mistaking this point. The people of the time assumed that religion was part of the daily lives in America. To think otherwise would be absurd.

No state mandated religion. Yet we are fully expected to be religious

We must put the relation of church and state into context. First, the Constitution does *not* state a total separation of church and state. However, the Constitution *does* specify that the government cannot mandate one religion over all the rest.

The United States is unique in that we allow all faiths to exist. In many other countries, the state mandates one religion. Churches of the other religions are destroyed, and people who continue to believe in those religions are put into prison. This is not so in America.

In America, you are allowed to believe in whatever religion you wish. You can build any church or temple, and no government will stop you. You can practice your beliefs, and no government will stop you. You are free to attend the services, to be spiritual and devoted in your own way, and no one will stop you.

That is what Freedom of Religion really means. Freedom of Religion means that you can be religious. You can practice your beliefs without any interference.

We are indeed expected to be religious, for religion is an important part of life. To live without religion of any kind is a difficult life indeed.

Note that all areas of the world have developed religious beliefs. This is because religion is such an important part of human existence. That is why it is very important for people to practice their religion freely—because religion is vital to the human experience.

We should also note that there are some universal truths to many religions, such as: knowing there is a spiritual world; knowing that there is something greater than ourselves; living ethically as this spiritual world wants us to; and relying on this spiritual world for inner peace and guidance.

From the pilgrims of the 1600s to the Americans of today, the American Way is a life of living religiously, in all of our affairs.

To repeat, Americans are expected to be religious. The Constitution states specifically that we have freedom of religion so that the government could not mandate a specific religion, and so that the government could not destroy all religions it did not like. However, the Founders fully expected the people to be religious.

Christianity and Judaism in American culture

Many people who discuss religious issues refer to a Judeo-Christian culture. Jewish and Christian religions have much in common, particularly the belief in God, and belief in common ethical principles. Thus combined, the total number of Americans with these similar views of God and moral beliefs is quite enormous.

America was founded primarily by Christians. We must remember that the pilgrims in the 1600s were mostly Christian. Furthermore, the religious views of the pilgrims and early colonists greatly influenced the Founding Fathers of the United States.

Centuries later, Christianity is still the most common religion in America. Even many of those who may not call themselves Christian are closely linked to it. For example, many Americans believe in a higher Being, and many agree with the teachings of Jesus.

Hence, the Judeo-Christian religions have a unique place in America.

However, unlike other nations or unlike other religions, Jews and Christians in America do NOT demand that this is the only religion. Many pilgrims were persecuted for their particular religion—even if it was merely a variation of Christianity. The colonials and Founding Fathers knew very well that we must have Freedom of Religion. This means that anyone can practice his religion without interference from the government.

Hence, although Christians in America created the principle of Freedom of Religion, they knew that this principle applied universally to all religions that exist.

However, in recent decades we have a problem. There are people who seek to destroy the Judeo-Christian religions. Remember, Christians were the ones who created Freedom of Religion in America. Also note that neither Christians nor Jews in America seek to destroy other religions. Why, then, are members of other religious beliefs trying to destroy the Judeo-Christian religions?

Further consequences of this attack on Judeo-Christian religions include the destruction of the people's rights to self-government and the people's right to live freely. In America we hold the principle of self-government. Thus, the majority of each community has the right to create laws and to set culture for their own community. If the majority of the people believe in Christianity, then they have the right to express themselves in that way. This principle would hold true for a community where the majority of people are Buddhists, Hindus, or of any other religion.

Hence, any community with the majority believing in a particular religion is allowed to believe and express themselves in that way. No person whose view is in the minority is allowed to dictate views to the majority.

The liberal-socialists must not force their religion on us

The liberal-socialists have been forcing their religious views on us. They must not do this.

The liberal-socialists do have a religion. They won't call it that, but it is a religious faith. Elements to their religion include: each individual is his own god; success at any cost without ethical concerns; hate anyone that talks of God; hate Christmas; stop any public display of religion (except for atheism and Islamic extremists); and make all other religions illegal.

These liberal-socialists are allowed to have their religious views. However, they are not allowed to make the rest of us adopt their views. They are not allowed to destroy all other religions so that their religion is the only one left.

This is precisely what the Amendment on Religious Freedom was designed to prevent.

Americans are a tolerant people. We have faiths from all parts of the world, and yet all faiths co-exist peacefully. If you travel as I have, you will see that this is a rarity. Americans are tolerant of other religions. We do not force you to join ours. This approach has been successful for hundreds of years.

In contrast, the liberal-socialists are not tolerant. They want their view, and only their view. They do the unthinkable. They want the state to mandate that their religious views are the only ones. They want to mandate, by law, that other religious faiths cannot exist.

This is extremely un-American. This is very intolerant. This is also unequivocally illegal, going against the Constitution.

Unfortunately, many of those in power do not see their actions as against the Constitution. Yet it could not be more clear.

Remember, the Constitution states specifically that the government cannot mandate a specific religion. The Constitution states that the government cannot destroy other religions that it did not like. However, that is precisely what many in the government are doing today.

Thus, we the people, as religious Americans, must continually clarify the Constitution. We must fight even the smallest intrusion on our religious freedoms, for the liberal-socialists will not stop until there is a state mandated religion. They will not stop until the socialist religion is the only religion allowed by law. To prevent this catastrophe, we must stop the liberal-socialists every time they step on our religious freedoms.

Add, never subtract

Part of the principle of Religious Freedom is that you can add elements of your religion, but you must never subtract others.

When you build a church of your faith, you do not have to tear down a church of a different faith. When you pray, you do not have to stop others from praying. When you read your religious books, you do not have to stop other people from reading theirs.

There is room in America for many religions, for many churches. In fact, if you look at many healthy communities, you will see several churches. Often times, churches of different faiths are built very close to each other. In America, all these faiths are allowed to co-exist, and exist close to each other, in peace and harmony. That doesn't happen in many other countries.

Thus, there is room for all faiths. Freedom of Religion allows any faith to grow and prosper. No one needs to tear down one religion in order to build theirs. More importantly, it is against the Constitution to do so.

Remember this principle: add yours—don't subtract others. Here are some specific ways this is done.
• Build your church. Do not destroy a church of a different faith.
• Encourage growth in your church. Do not slander or hurt people of other faiths.
• Add the prayers of your faith to the prayers that currently exist in the community, such at schools and at community functions. Do not deny the rest of the community their right to pray in their own way at these times.
• Add your own plaques of religious laws from your own faith to public parks and courthouses. Do not force the removal of plaques of other faiths. Don't force the removal of any statements which the community wants. All religious principles can be placed side by side.

To repeat: add—don't subtract. It is morally wrong to take away the religious expressions of the community. Furthermore, to take away any religious expression is clearly and unequivocally un-Constitutional.

Instead of denying people their Right, instead of denying the community things that they want, add yours. Add your prayers. Add your religious books. Add your plaques. Build your churches. All these public displays of religion can exist peacefully side by side. That is the American Way.

Being a minority in a particular religious culture

This section is written directly to the person who holds a different religious view than the majority of the community. This message is particularly addressed to Atheists and those opposed to God.

Remember, America is unique in that anyone is allowed to practice his religion. There is no religion of the "wrong type" that is persecuted. That is key. The fact that you are in the minority is *not* the same as being persecuted for being in the minority.

In other countries, one religion is the only religion, and all others are forbidden. People of those other faiths are often killed in those countries. This is very different from America, where you happen to be in the minority, a mere statistical issue, yet you are still allowed to practice your beliefs.

If you are of a minority faith, follow these rules:

1. You do not have the right to stop others from practicing their religion.

If the majority in the community believe in a religion, and enjoy it, then they have a right to do it. Freedom of Religion gives them that right, and you have no right to stop them.

2. You do not have the right to impose your religion on others.

You may have your own beliefs. However, you are never allowed to force your beliefs as the only ones.

3. Ignore public words of religion.

When someone talks of religion, or makes a prayer you don't like, just ignore it. When you say the Pledge of Allegiance, just don't say "under God." When someone says a prayer at the beginning of a football game, go get a snack—it will be over in about 30 seconds. Ignore it, let everyone else enjoy it, and get on with life.

4. Practice your religion, but don't force it on us

You may practice your religion as you please. You can do as you please at home and in your church. You are allowed to pray in private, to read religious books on your faith, or to have discussions with fellow men about your religion. America does not deny you any of this.

However, you cannot force your religion on us. We, too, are allowed to pray in private, to practice our religion at home, and to discuss our religion in public. Both religions exist—yours and mine. I practice religion my way, you practice it yours. I express myself my way, you express yourself in yours. Yet one cannot dictate to another. In America, both are allowed to exist equally.

5. Add, don't subtract

Add your own statements and your own prayers. We will let you have your views on equal time with ours, if it is that important to you. However, you can never deny the rest of the community their rights. You must never take away any element of religious speech. That act is unequivocally illegal.

What religious people can do in America

Religious people in America *can* do things. Americans have been told otherwise by the religious left. I hereby give Americans permission to do these things—it is your Constitutional Right.

Americans are allowed to:

- •pray silently at school or work
- •read the Bible on your own time
- •bless the meal at civic luncheons
- •open legislatures with a prayer
- •pray before playing a sport
- •put "In God We Trust" on our currency
- •give thanks before every meal
- •have religious signs on your car
- •religious quotations or calendars
- •open courts with a prayer
- •talk about Christmas at work
- •have "under God" in the Pledge
- •Post the Ten Commandments in public places
- •Public displays of Christmas—such as parks, streets, and govt. buildings
- •Speak about God or quote scriptures, in casual conversation or at work
- •Hold informal religious gatherings at home
- •Celebrate each religious holiday, in private or at a church, in your own way

This list is not exhaustive; there are many more acts that religious Americans have a right to do.

Summary

Basic Truth of America: Freedom of Religion means Freedom to Be Religious.

America was founded by people who believed in God. Even today, most Americans believe in God. People may have different concepts of God, yet many Americans acknowledge the existence of some type of God.

We do not separate God from government. However, the government is not allowed to dictate one religion over others. The government cannot destroy any religion, for all religions must be allowed and tolerated.

In addition, *individuals* must also be tolerant of differing religious views. Individuals must also remember that tolerance must go both ways—you must be as tolerant of my beliefs as I am of yours.

In America we have Freedom of Religion. This means that each American is free to practice his religious beliefs without persecution from the government.

Being of a minority religion is a mere statistical fact, not a conspiracy. Unlike in other countries, even if you are the minority religion in your community, you are still allowed to practice your beliefs. However, by the same principle, you cannot dictate your religion to others.

Add, don't subtract. You may build your churches, say your prayers, and have your public displays of religion. However, you must never remove a religious item or prohibit anyone from expressing their religious beliefs. Any act of removing or prohibiting religious expression is illegal, clearly in opposition to the U.S. Constitution.

Americans do not separate religion from life. Many people believe that religion is central to a good life, not just in America, but throughout the world, and throughout the centuries. Freedom of religion is so important because religion is such a vital part of the human experience. With this freedom, men are allowed to live their religion as they choose, and are allowed let their religion guide them through life.

We will see in other chapters how religion in America is a vital, positive factor in America's greatness.

Freedom, Responsibility, and Ethics

With our Rights and Freedoms also come Responsibility and Ethics. These items cannot be separated.

Too many people misunderstand Freedom and Rights. Freedom does *not* allow you to do anything; there are limits. Common misconceptions include: you are not responsible for your actions; you do not have to be ethical if you are truly free; and you do not have to be a responsible citizen to be worthy of your rights.

In brief the <u>truths</u> are: an American is responsible for his actions and his choices; an American must live ethically at all times; an American should sometimes curtail his own freedoms for the benefit of the community; and an American needs to be a responsible citizen if he wants to be worthy of his rights.

An American is free to make choices. However he must take responsibility for all of his decisions. His choices should always be ethical.

<u>Freedom and Responsibility</u>

<u>Responsibility for self</u>
1 A man must be responsible for taking care of himself.
2. A man must be responsible for earning his own income.
3. A man must be responsible for the decisions he makes.
4. A man must admit to his mistakes and own his failures.
5. A man must take responsibility for any illegal or unethical act.

Responsibility in the community

1. A man must be a good neighbor in his community.
2. A man must be an intelligent and informed voter.
3. A man should take active part in self-government.
4. A man should be a responsible juror when called.
5. A man must work to improve his community on a regular basis.

Freedom and Ethics

1. A man must not slander the good name of a fellow American.
2. A man must not get money by taking it from another man.
3. A man must be honest and fair in all his activities.
4. A man must never use his freedom in a way which hurts another.
5. A man must sometimes compromise his freedoms, understanding that neighbors may have different competing desires.
6. A man must realize that his freedom ends where another man's property and personal space begins.

A more detailed discussion of ethics can be found in the respective areas of other chapters.

Summary

Proper use of our Freedoms must include responsibility, ethics, and choices. We must be responsible for ourselves and our decisions. We must be ethical in all areas in order to deserve our Freedoms. We must be responsible for governing our nation, and be responsible for taking care of our communities.

PART III
Religion in the United States

Founding Fathers Were Religious

Many people came to America to practice their religion freely. Then in the Revolutionary times, the Founding Fathers of the United States clearly lived and governed while knowing God.

In the early days of the Colonies, up to the Revolution, there was a general spiritual movement throughout the land. This movement not only talked of God and morals, but also of self-government and freedoms.

The line between clergy and political activists was quite blurred in those days. Clergy talked of freedoms and independence, while political leaders spoke of God in their speeches as an accepted fact. God was part of all aspects of life. The Colonials and Revolutionaries would never agree to separate God from life in the way many people push for today.

Patrick Henry

Patrick Henry, in his famous speech of "Give me liberty or give me death!" talks of God, and does so several times.

"It is only in this way that we can hope to arrive at the truth and fulfill the great responsibility which we hold to *God* and our country...I repeat sir, we must fight. An appeal to arms and to the *God of Hosts* is all that is left us...Sir, we are not weak, if we make a proper use of the means which the *God* of nature hath placed in our power...There is a *just God* who presides over the destinies of nations, and who will raise friends to fight our battles for us...Why stand we here idle? What is it that gentlemen wish? What would they have? Is life so dear, or peace so sweet, as to be purchased at the price of chains and slavery? Forbid it, *Almighty God!* I know not what course others may take, but as for me: Give me liberty, or give me death!" (italics added)

Thomas Jefferson

Thomas Jefferson talks of God in the Declaration of Independence: "...that they are endowed by their *Creator* with certain unalienable Rights..." The Declaration further states in the final paragraph: "And for the support of this Declaration, *with a firm reliance on the protection of Divine Providence*, we mutually pledge to each other our Lives, our Fortunes and our sacred Honor." (italics added)

James Madison

James Madison is known as the Father of our Constitution, and for good reason. It was Madison who studied many governments of the past, and it was Madison who came up with many basic components of our Constitution.

James Madison had this to say about self-government and God: "We have staked the whole of all our political institutions upon the capacity of mankind for self-government, upon the capacity of each and all of us to govern ourselves, to control ourselves, and to sustain ourselves according to the Ten Commandments of God."

Ben Franklin

Ben Franklin firmly believed in God. Franklin is in many ways the ultimate ideal of the American: scientist, philosopher, successful businessman, diplomat, and much more. This man was highly successful, very famous, and believed in God.

In his autobiography, Franklin talks of his views on religion. Here are just a few of his views: "I never doubted, for instance, the existence of the Deity; that there is one God, who made all things; that he ought to be worshipped by adoration, prayer, and thanksgiving; that the most acceptable service of God is doing good to man; that the soul is immortal; and that God will certainly reward virtue and punish vice, either here or hereafter."

Franklin also wrote his own prayer, which he used daily: "O powerful Goodness! bountiful Father! merciful Guide: Increase in me that wisdom which discovers my truest interest. Strengthen my resolutions to perform what that wisdom dictates. Accept my kind offices to thy other children as the only return in my power for thy continual favors to me."

Ben Franklin was a famous man, even in his own time. Franklin was very successful, having created, discovered, and achieved many great things in his life. This quintessential American believed, without doubt, in the existence of God, and it is likely that there is a correlation between his religious views and his very successful life.

George Washington

George Washington also believed in God. A clear example is when Washington as President set aside Thanksgiving Day as a celebration for the United States.

First, we must always remember, that Thanksgiving is giving thanks to God for our blessings. That fact alone is an acceptance of God in American culture from the very beginning.

Further, note how often Washington mentions God in his proclamation. Here is the full text of Washington's proclamation setting aside a day for Thanksgiving. I have emphasized each reference to God in order to bring it closer to your attention.

New York, 3 October 1789
By the President of the United States of America. a Proclamation.

"Whereas it is the duty of all Nations to acknowledge the <u>providence of Almighty God</u>, <u>to obey his will</u>, <u>to be grateful for his benefits</u>, and <u>humbly to implore his protection and favor</u>—and whereas both Houses of Congress have by their joint Committee requested me 'to recommend to the People of the United States a day of <u>public thanksgiving and prayer</u> to be observed by acknowledging with grateful hearts <u>the many signal favors of</u> <u>Almighty God</u> especially by affording them an opportunity peaceably to establish a form of government for their safety and happiness.'"

"Now therefore I do recommend and assign Thursday the 26th day of November next to be devoted by the People of these States <u>to the service of that</u>

great and glorious Being, who is the beneficent Author of all the good that was, that is, or that will be—That we may then all unite in rendering unto him our sincere and humble thanks—for his kind care and protection of the People of this Country previous to their becoming a Nation—for the signal and manifold mercies, and the favorable interpositions of his Providence which we experienced in the tranquility, union, and plenty, which we have since enjoyed—for the peaceable and rational manner, in which we have been enabled to establish constitutions of government for our safety and happiness, and particularly the national One now lately instituted—for the civil and religious liberty with which we are blessed; and the means we have of acquiring and diffusing useful knowledge; and in general for all the great and various favors which he hath been pleased to confer upon us."

"And also that we may then unite in most humbly offering our prayers and supplications to the great Lord and Ruler of Nations and beseech him to pardon our national and other transgressions—to enable us all, whether in public or private stations, to perform our several and relative duties properly and punctually—to render our national government a blessing to all the people, by constantly being a Government of wise, just, and constitutional laws, discreetly and faithfully executed and obeyed—to protect and guide all Sovereigns and Nations (especially such as have shewn kindness onto us) and to bless them with good government, peace, and concord—To promote the knowledge and practice of true religion and virtue, and the increase of science among them and us—and generally to grant unto all Mankind such a degree of temporal prosperity as he alone knows to be best."

"Given under my hand at the City of New-York the third day of October in the year of our Lord 1789."

Washington

Washington fought for our right to self-government. He believed in self-government so much that he refused to be crowned king, nor even President for life. Instead, Washington stepped down after two terms so that the people could freely choose their next President. What better man then to look at regarding the relationships of self-government, God, and America? It is clear that this Father of our country believed in God. It is clear that for all his deeds, the Father of our country acknowledged another father for his blessings—the Father in Heaven.

Other people

From the days of the Pilgrims to the formation of the United States, religion played an important role in the lives and in the civic affairs of most Americans. If you look at the letters, documents, and speeches of the time, it is clear that the people believed in God as an accepted fact.

Summary

The Founding Fathers believed in God. The common people of the various colonies were devoted to God. They were devoted to God; they knew that He was greater than any man. They knew that we should be humble and be thankful to Him. They knew that good government comes not just from wise men, but from wise men who are virtuous, and who ask God for His guidance and blessings.

The men and women who worked to create this country would surely tell us that devotion to God must be a central part of our lives. They would think it folly to act otherwise.

Government and Religion: Self-government does not exclude God

Remember that we said that in America the people govern themselves. Remember that we also said that there are two manifestations of self-government: 1. The people control their own lives, and 2. The people control the government.

These issues of self-government are specified in contrast to being governed by another person, such as by a dictator or king. However, self-government does not say anything about excluding God. In fact, whether we are talking about one's personal life, or whether we are talking about the people controlling the government, the best examples of self-government always include a relationship with God.

Just as when we examined the two manifestations of self-government earlier, we can clarify this new issue through examining the two manifestations of self-government *when it involves God*. These are: 1. The people control their own lives, with guidance from God, and 2. The people control the government, with guidance from God.

1. <u>The people control their own lives, with guidance from God</u>

God has given us free will. In one sense, that means that He gives us the choice to do anything. Yet, that is not to say that all acts are acceptable. Nevertheless, God allows us to make those choices.

Similarly, the U.S. Constitution gives individuals freedoms. Each person is free to pursue his happiness, to make mistakes, and to reap rewards of his labor. Yet, that is not to say that all acts are acceptable. Nevertheless, the U.S. Constitution allows us to make those choices.

God does not demand compliance, but he wants it. God does not demand we come to Him, but He wants us with Him. He is always available and will always welcome us.

So, although the U.S. Constitution gives us Freedoms, and God gave us a free will to choose, it is always better that we make the choice to be with God. When we choose to be with God, we are guided by Him. With His guidance, we are better people. This translates into everything good—better health, greater career success, more cooperative communities, and more personal happiness.

As I see it, you may control your own life, but you should ask God for guidance. Some people say that this should be taken further, that it is best to give up control of your life totally and let God control your life completely. I'm not certain about that issue. However, I do know that self-government *without* God in your life will enable you to go only so far, whereas self-government *with* God in your life will enable you to blossom to a much greater degree.

To summarize: The U.S. Constitution allows Americans a great range of freedoms and choices. We are allowed to make many choices for our lives without hindrance from other men. Yet, at the same time, if we have a relationship with God, and we ask for guidance from Him, then our choices will be that much better. These guided choices will make us better people and enable us to have better relationships. These guided choices will make us happier, make us more successful, and make our lives richer.

2. The people control the government, with guidance from God

In America, the people control the government. Those who write the laws are elected by the people, to work on behalf of the people. The people govern themselves in civic matters, from city councils, to the President.

This stands in direct contrast to a dictatorship. In a dictatorship, the one dictator makes the laws, without any input from the people. This is what makes our system unique—in civic matters, the people govern themselves.

However, this self-government is only in contrast to a dictator. There is nothing in the self-government principle that excludes asking for guidance. That is indeed what the best American leaders do—they ask for guidance from God.

When the President takes his solemn oath of office, he does so with his hand on the Bible. The final words of his oath are usually "So help me God." This is no accident. The President knows the awesome responsibility that he has been given. He knows he could use all the help from above that he can.

It is no accident that many legislatures throughout America start their day with a prayer. It is no accident that many courts in America also start their day with a prayer. These bodies know that their actions have consequences of great influence. Men in these governing bodies ask God for guidance, so that they are more able to make the best judgments on behalf of the people.

Every US coin and paper currency bears the words "In God We Trust." The words could not be simpler or more clear. Yes, we the people run the governments of the nation, yes we run our individual lives, but in all this self-government, we put our trust in God.

Notice that the words do *not* read "In Congress We Trust", "In the President We Trust" nor even "In the spirit of Jefferson and Washington We Trust." No, the words are "In God We Trust" and the words mean exactly that.

Irving Berlin understood the relationship of God and America well. In his song "God Bless America", Irving Berlin wrote these fine lyrics: "Stand beside her, and guide her, through the night with a light from above."

"Guidance"—this is a primary principle in governing ourselves. Yes, we are free from kings and dictators. Yes, we are free to gather and make judgments for the betterment of all. Yet, we should always ask for guidance from the "light from above." Only through a deep relationship with God, and asking for guidance from a being so much greater than ourselves, will we be able to make the best decisions.

Summary

Government is not separate from religion. An individual life is not separate from religion. These things were never intended to be separate from religion, and never should be.

The better leaders of our nation know that good self-government requires a deep relationship with the spiritual world. Self-government allows us to make many choices, but it is only with guidance from the spiritual world that we will be able to make *good* choices. Only with guidance from above will we be able to govern ourselves well.

We are a church going people

The Constitution gives us freedoms, but religion keeps us grounded and doing what is right. Our church going culture makes us better individuals, helps communities remain strong, and gives us hope. Our religious nature helps us use our freedoms wisely.

Most Americans go to church. Even when Americans are not regular church goers, they believe in God, they pray, and they read religious books. This church-going activity is a deeply rooted part of the American culture.

Positive effect of religions in general

A good religion will have four main items:

1. Belief in a spiritual world, which focuses on things beyond us and more important than ourselves.
2. Moral fabric, with rules and lifestyles which help us to live in a way which is better for us.
3. Community, where humans can share in joys and sorrows of life, and where people can help each other.
4. Hope, faith, and guidance, helping us make difficult choices, and giving us strength through difficult times.

1. Belief in God and spiritual world

There is a God. Americans can have different interpretations of what God is like, but there is a higher being. America's religious nature acknowledges God.

Men who acknowledge the existence of God and a spiritual world behave very differently from those men who think there is no God or spiritual world. A man's view of life and how to live it is greatly altered depending on which view he holds.

We will look at a few of these differences and their practical effects throughout this chapter.

Hence, our belief in a God and spiritual world has greatly influenced our American history and culture. The American Way, in a variety of aspects, is related to the church-going nature of the American people.

2. Morals, Religion, and America's Greatness

America can only be a great nation if the people are grounded in morals. Going to church helps Americans do just that. It is true that there are men who are moral and yet not religious; however, this is the exception not the rule.

Americans must have ethics. Only by living ethically will our communities be healthy and our businesses be prosperous. Only by living ethically will individuals be satisfied and at peace with themselves.

It is because we believe in God and because we go to church that we remain ethical. It is our religious ways that enable us to be good people, and it is because we are good people that we have a great nation.

There is a direct correlation between going to church and ethical standards. Where people are church going, the ethical standards are high. Pick an area and you will find studies which prove this to be true.

Furthermore, ethical standards directly affect the quality of life in America. Again, pick any area of life—education, government, business—and you will find studies which prove this to be true. Businesses are much more profitable when they act ethically. Government operates best for the people when the government workers are ethical. Schools offer a much better quality of education when the schools believe in ethics. To repeat: there is a direct correlation between church-going, ethics, and quality.

The converse holds true as well. Wherever religion is subtracted from an area of life, we see that ethics fall dramatically, and, as a consequence, the quality of the organization suffers. Be it a personal life, in schools, in businesses, or in government, dropping religion results in substantially decreased quality of the organization. Pick any area, and you will find studies which show this to be true. To repeat: there exists a direct correlation between church-going, ethics, and quality.

There are several reasons why a going to church helps us live better.

a) The universal ethical principles are ancient, however humans need constant reminding. Reading the Bible, listening to sermons, and being involved in church activities all serve to remind us what is too easy to forget.

b) In addition, it is easier to be moral by going to church. Living the ethical path can be difficult. However, with a community of people trying to live by the same standards, it is easier for all to be ethical. Each member helps the others to stay on the path.

c) Finally, God Himself helps us to be moral. God has given us rules to live by—which are really for our own good. Many people speak of having a healthy fear of God, and that is what keeps them on the right path. In addition, many people find that appealing to God, the Higher Being, is an important way to get strength to do what is right even in the most trying of circumstances.

To repeat: our church-going nature is essential to keeping us ethical, and, we must be ethical in order to function best as a society. The Constitution gives us freedom, but our religious views keep us behaving wisely. In turn, freedoms combined with ethics make America a great nation.

3. Community and religion

A church is not just a place to worship; it is a place for a community to grow.

We need each other for survival, for coping with life. We need a strong community spirit to help each other as individuals, and to help our neighborhood as a whole. The church is a natural center to link American communities.

Furthermore, several bad trends have occurred in the last decades, all of which are related to a decrease in religious activities. These include: fewer people attend church regularly; neighbors know other neighbors less; people long for a sense of community that seems to no longer exist; and the government is taking over more and more social services. This is not the way of America. When the church going culture declines, a landslide of other problems fall with it. People may not think these items are related, but they are.

America's church-going culture is a deeply rooted part of America's culture of community spirit. When you go to church, you join a community. You will find that you know your neighbors much better. When you need help, there will be fellow men and women in the congregation who will help you out. The church even helps the community, and, as an additional benefit government programs are not necessary.

Churches have always been centers of the community. This church-going culture naturally lends itself to a stronger community spirit.

4. Faith, hope, religion, and American optimism

Going to church also gives Americans faith and hope. Americans who are church going are more optimistic about life. They are enthusiastic. This optimism and enthusiasm makes these Americans more successful. It makes them much happier. A further benefit is that their enthusiasm is infective to others in the community.

Most important, as serious troubles come along, religion helps us cope. Church going people face these troubles more easily than those who are not religious. Faith, hope, and prayer give strength to many people in the most desperate of circumstances.

Note that church going people are *not* free from trouble. The difference, however, is that their religious beliefs give them more strength than those who don't believe.

America's can-do attitude is unique among the world, and is also linked to our church-going nature. America's religious beliefs include hope and faith. This translates into areas which seem unrelated to religion. Americans believe in achieving the impossible. Americans believe in trying new things. Americans have faith that tomorrow will be better than today, and a tragedy of today will be survived through to tomorrow. America's optimism, can-do attitude, and overall faith are unique in the world. It is in part due to our church-going culture that

America has this attitude, and it is in part due to this church-going culture that keeps this American optimism alive.

Summary

Americans are a church going people. We always have gone to church, and we always will. Although the Constitution guarantees our Freedoms, it is our church-going nature that keeps Americans going the right direction. It is our religious foundation and deeply rooted religious beliefs which help us use our freedoms wisely, and thus really make our country great.

We are a nation of self-government, but that implies we can govern ourselves. Our religious nature keeps us focused on what is right and good. Because we are focused on being good, then we can govern our lives better.

Our church-going nature gives people faith and hope. It is a center of communities, linking neighbors together. It encourages people to live wisely, whether on a personal level or in the government.

Whenever church-going people are involved in an organization, the quality and success of the organization is great. Wherever religion is dropped, the quality of the organization and community drops too. Church-going is deeply rooted in our American culture, and actually provides many vital ingredients to America's greatness.

Christmas in America— the Universal Holiday

Christmas is both a religious holiday and a non-religious holiday. Christmas is in many ways a universal holiday.

Charles Dickens describes Christmas well in one paragraph of his novel, *A Christmas Carol.*

"There are many things from which I might have derived good, by which I have not profited, I dare say," returned the nephew: "Christmas among the rest. But I am sure I have always thought of Christmas time, when it has come round—apart from the veneration due to its sacred name and origin, if anything belonging to it can be apart from that—as a good time: a kind, forgiving, charitable, pleasant time: the only time I know of, in the long calendar year, when men and women seem by one consent to open their shut-up hearts freely, and to think of the people below them as if they really were fellow-passengers to the grave, and not another race of creatures bound on other journeys. And therefore, uncle, though it has never put a scrap of gold or silver in my pocket, I believe that it *has* done me good; and I say, God bless it!"

Christmas, by its name, is a celebration of the birth of Christ. To that extent, it is a religious holiday. Christians know this and they don't forget it. However, there is a much more universal appeal to Christmas than just the religious celebrations. Dickens knew this, and so had his character say it. Americans have known this as well. Christmas in America has evolved into many good things, and evolved into many universal celebrations of the human spirit, which are distinct from the specific religious elements.

Christmas is a good time. It is indeed the one time in the year when men and women are more friendly and forgiving to each other. It is the time to renew friendships, get closer to families, to be kind to strangers. Christmas is the time to take a deep breath, and remember what the most important things in life really are.

We are busy, and we don't always have the time to spend with family and friends. Then, too, life is difficult. Your job is tough, the kids get sick, the car breaks down...sometimes you tend to go crazy. The Christmas season is the one time when for a full month out of the year we cool our temper, we are more forgiving, and we are more loving. We are kinder and more joyful. Christmas is an important annual relief from realities. It is a necessary spiritual breath, and a reminder of all that we should be grateful for.

Why are certain Christmas stories so popular? Christmas stories are popular because they are so universal. Tales such as *A Christmas Carol*, and *It's a Wonderful Life* are tales not just of Christmas, but of the human spirit. They are not stories of religion, but stories of the heart.

Christmas is really a universal holiday because it is a celebration of universal truths. It is the time for friends and family, it is the time for loving and forgiving, it is the time for songs and feasts. Christmas is a time to be thankful for all the good things you have. It is the time to remember what life is about, and renewing your dedication to it.

I suggest that men and women of all faiths, even atheists, adopt Christmas. As for myself, I considered myself atheist for many years, and I did not grow up in a church going family. Yet, not a year went by when I did not celebrate Christmas—and I am glad of that. Whatever your religious beliefs are, embrace the Christmas holiday season as it is celebrated in America. Enjoy public displays of Christmas decorations and Christmas cheer. Renew friendships, be kind and generous, and enjoy the Christmas stories. During this season, remember what a good life is really about.

Christmas is indeed a good time, a charitable time, the only time when busy people open their hearts again and renew their friendships. And I say, God bless it.

Summary of Religion, Government, and America

This topic is important enough to have a separate chapter summary. You will rarely find these concepts in textbooks or talked about by academics. Here are some key points:

1. <u>Separation of Church and State is a myth</u>

The Constitution does not say anywhere that church must be separate from state.

In fact, the Founding Fathers fully intended us to include religion with our government. Look at their speeches and documents and you will find it very clear that God was a central part to their lives and to the way they ran the government. Therefore, any part of government CAN mention religion or God.

What the concept of separation of church and state says is that the government is not allowed to demand one religion over all the rest. Also remember that this concept, though a good one, is not even stated in the Constitution. It is discussed in other historical documents.

The United States never has, and never will, dictate one religion over another. If you want to see real government dictating religion, look at other nations. If you want to see true religious persecution, not the fabricated tales that socialists tell about America, then look at other countries.

Look at Communist countries and Islamic countries. See what the pilgrims left and why they came here. Those are examples of the government dictating religion. Those are examples of where there is no separation of church and state. Go read your history, go visit those current dictatorships, then come back here and compare. The United States is nothing like that at all. Here in America, the government does not dictate religion. There is a big difference between America and many other nations regarding religious freedom.*

*The only exception, of course, is the socialists who are working to destroy all religions in America. The only people dictating religion today are the socialists, who are working to remove every mention of God, and to deny the people their religious freedoms. However, this is not part of the American principles. These people are clearly in the wrong, are clearly going against the Constitution, and should be fired or jailed for their actions.

2. God is an inclusive concept

God means a higher being. All peoples of the world have some concept of a god, of a spiritual being. Even many who don't believe in God think of the spiritual world. For example, New Age religions rely on listening to the heart, or the God within. Other religions think of a spiritual world in the plants and animals, and rely on this collective spirit for peace and guidance. Even Atheists can take the concept of God and make it their inner heart.

Note that of all those religions that believe in God, there is not one religion that is singled out as being better, or the only religion. "God" can be the God as understood by any of those religions.

The concept of God, and the word God, are so inclusive that there is not one person in America who should be offended. Furthermore, because the people get to decide what they want, and the great majority of people want God in public documents and activities, that God must be allowed to stay in government and must be allowed to stay in public places.

You can think of God in your own terms, but there is no reason at all to get rid of God in any form in our public lives. In the United States, God must stay. As a side note to atheists: remember, I was once an Atheist myself, and I had no problem with the God concept in public America. God should stay in the public areas, if for no other reason than because the majority of people want God to stay in the public areas.

3. Freedom of Religion means the Freedom to be Religious

We have the right to worship any way we wish. We have the right to have any beliefs we want. This is one of the primary fundamental rights of being an American. We are allowed this freedom in full. Regardless of what anyone else may tell you, this Freedom of Religion is allowed to stay. We, the people, are allowed to be religious in any way we want.

Many of the early settlers of America came here precisely because of religious freedom. They escaped persecution to practice freely as they wanted.

The Founding Fathers were deeply religious, and assumed government and religion would be linked. Yet they wanted to practice religion in their own way—hence they put in the Religious Freedom phrase into the First Amendment. Still, that means people are free to practice religion as they choose—which implies that the people will fully be religious, and that the government has no right to stop it.

A fundamental American principle is that the people have a right to do and believe as they wish. Thus, if the majority of people wish to be religious, then they have a right to be religious.

For all these reasons, the people have a full right to be religious in this country. Freedom of Religion does not mean freedom from religion, but rather the freedom to be religious. Any man or organization that interferes with this right must be stopped, for such an action is illegal and un-Constitutional.

4. Being a minority is a statistic, not a conspiracy

The majority of Americans are Christian or Jewish. That's just the way it is.

If you happen to believe in a religion that is in the minority in your community, that is okay. It is not a conspiracy, it is just a numbers issue.

There is a big difference between America and other countries. In other countries, you would be forced to adopt the religious views of the majority. However, in America we let you believe and worship as you want. In other countries, the government would destroy your church. However, in America the government will let you keep any church building you want. In other countries you may be arrested, tortured, or killed for having the wrong religious belief. In America, we don't care—you can believe whatever you want and not worry about harm.

So you see, being a minority in religious views does not prohibit you here in America. No one pushes their religion on you, no one forces you to go to their church, no one stops you from going to your own church—you are free to worship as you wish. The fact that you are in the minority is just statistics; in some other city you may find more who believe like you.

There is no conspiracy. You can believe as you wish, even if your religious beliefs are a tiny minority of the community. However, by the same principle, you must allow others to practice their religion as they wish. That is the big difference between the Untied States and many other countries.

PART IV

Economics and Success in America

Free Market Economy and Running Your Own Business

<u>Free Market Economy</u>

The economic system in America is based on the Free Market Economy. This means that everyone may trade their goods and services on the open market, seeking as much profit as they want.

The people are free to make any product they want, offer any service they want, and ask any price they want. The buyers are then free to buy the product or service they want. The most popular products and services will sell the best, the companies which sell those items will become the wealthiest, and the employees of those companies will prosper the most.

It is in this way that each American can get the goods and services he wants. It is in this way that each American can become as rich as he wants.

<u>Advantages to the Free Market Economy</u>

1. Each person can have exactly the goods and services he wants.
2. There is no shortage, and there is less waiting.
3. The quality of each product is the best it can be.
4. The price will be the lowest cost it can be.
5. Any American can become as rich as he wants.
6. Creativity and progress occurs easily.

We will discuss each of these.

1. Each person can have exactly the goods and services he wants.

With a free market economy, if someone wants a product, he can find it or make it. If someone wants a service, he can find someone who will do it, or start this service as a business himself. Therefore, there is never any limit to the range of goods and services available.

Other economic systems, such as socialism, do not allow the people all the products they want. Only the free market system provides the incentive for creative individuals and wise businessmen to make the goods and services that the people want.

2. There is no shortage, and there is less waiting.

The free market uses the concepts of supply and demand. If the people need more of a product, then a smart businessman will make more of that product. If one business is already producing at capacity, a second person will open up a business and provide the needed goods. (And in the process, all businessmen will thrive).

There will never be a shortage of goods that people want, for businesses will provide them. There will rarely be waiting, for businesses will step up production to meet demand.

Other economic systems, such as socialism, often fail to provide enough goods to the people. No government, even the United States government, can predict supply and demand. Only with the free market economy can local companies quickly meet local needs, and thus ensure that communities will never have a shortage of goods.

3. The quality of each product is the best it can be.

The free market economy is competitive. It is true that anyone can provide a product or service, but if the people don't like it, then the company must improve the quality of what it offers or it will go out of business. By necessity of survival, all companies are forced to make the best product they can. This is important for the consumer, for he always has a choice of the best quality goods and services.

Other economic systems, such as socialism, do not have incentive for quality products. Only the free market system provides that incentive.

4. The price will be the lowest cost it can be.

Competition applies to cost as well. It is true that anyone can ask any price for his product or service, but if the people don't want to pay it, then the company will go out of business.

Someone will always provide a product of equal quality at a cheaper price. By necessity of survival, all companies are forced to make not only the best product they can, but make it as cheaply as they can. This is important for the consumer, for then he can afford more goods and services.

This has two results. First, the individuals can have more goods, and are much more satisfied in their lives. Second, when a consumer buys more goods, he is keeping more businesses alive, and thus helps more individuals like himself to prosper.

Other economic systems, such as socialism, do not have any incentive for being cost effective. Only the free market system provides the incentive to keep costs down.

5. Any American can become as rich as he wants.

The free market economy is like a race—may the best man win. If a man has a greatly superior product, or works especially hard to make his product popular, then he may earn an unlimited amount of money.

In a free market system, any man, no matter what his background is, can become as wealthy as wants to be.

Other economic systems, such as socialism, do not allow this individual success. Only the free market economy does.

6. Creativity and progress occurs easily.

If there is no incentive, then why change? Most people will be creative or change only when there is reason. Free Market Economy provides an excellent reason.

Suppose a man invents a new product, something different that no one else has done. The people want it—right now he's the only one who has it—and so he becomes successful.

Companies that already exist must change. They must find new products, and new services. Companies are forced to improve by the competition in the free market economy.

Other economic systems, such as socialism, do not have incentive for new ideas. Only the free market system provides that incentive. Thus, with the incentive of a free market economy, innovation and progress occurs much more often than with other economic systems.

Contrasting economic system: Socialism

The major contrasting economic system to the free market economy is socialism.

We must be clear in our understanding that: 1) socialism is not consistent with American principles, and 2) socialism is an absolute path to economic disaster.

In socialism, the government runs the economy. This is the central point behind socialism. The problem is that even with the best intentions, no government can run the economy. Even individual businesses are not always correct on how much product to make, or which new products the people will want. If the most successful businesses have this difficulty, how can a government do any better? How can a national government make decisions for all products and all services in an entire nation? Clearly, the government cannot effectively operate a national economy.

Socialism has failed everywhere it has been tried. Here are but a few of the economic disasters that come from a socialist economy:

1. Shortages. Socialist nations have shortages in everything, including basic needs such as bread. The former USSR was infamous for its bread lines.

2. Not getting products people want. People may want products, such as those in America, but the people cannot get them. The government won't allow it.

3. Poor quality products and services. Because there is no competition in socialist nations, there is no incentive to do better. The people do minimal work in making products, and the service industries have no reason to improve. Socialized health care is one of the most abysmal examples of the poor quality arising from socialized services.

4. A class system. There are really two classes in socialist nations: the elite, and the masses. The elite are paid well, live in nice homes, and have all the food and comforts they need. The masses are given just enough, but not much more.

5. No chance for success. In socialist nations, there is no chance for a man to become rich. There is no chance for a man to become truly successful.

Running Your Own Business

One of the greatest things about America is that anyone can start a business.

When you own your own business, you are self-reliant. You are not beholden to anyone. That is a feeling of self-reliance and freedom like no other.

Furthermore, because America is the land of opportunity, anyone can do it. There is nothing stopping you from starting your own little business and making a comfortable living.

There are many mistaken people in America who think that starting a business is impossible. Too many people think that life is just to complex for individualism, that the pioneering spirit worked fine a hundred years ago, but this cannot exist today. This is absolutely not true. You can be just as much a pioneer and a business owner today as in any time in our history.

Local examples

I will give a few examples. Note that these are not merely hypothetical examples. I am thinking of real people I know, from communities throughout America, who have started their own business and been very successful.

Examples of small businesses Americans have started and own themselves: Restaurant—of all types, construction company, grocery store, trucking company, import-export service, laundry service, local newspaper, radio station, web design, computer repair, dentistry, optometry, flower shop, tax accounting, hotel service, bed and breakfast, furniture moving, photography, dance studio, martial arts instruction, taxi cab, limo service, auto repair shop, ethnic specialty food store, farming, ranching, health food store, bakery, and many, many more.

I know specific people in each of these professions who started their own business and are doing quite well. None of these are technology businesses. None of these Americans were born into the wealthy elite. These people just used their talents and followed their interests to create their business. They created a product they liked for themselves, and developed a business that was in line with their passions.

Some were even immigrants, barely knowing the American culture or language. In some cases, the business has gone through several generations. In some cases, the owners have built a chain of several stores in the area. In other cases they own just one store, but that is enough—for owning just one store gives these people a good income, as well as a full life of independence and pride.

There are thousands of successful small business stories in this country just like the few that I mentioned. Each day, hundreds more people start their own entrepreneurial dream. You could be one of them.

How to start your own business

You say you don't know how to start a business? You don't know the first thing to do? Here's the secret: talk to your chamber of commerce.

Each city has a chamber of commerce. Even most of the smaller towns have one. The chamber has people who can help you to get your business going. The purposes of most chambers are two things: to promote economic vitality, and to ensure quality of life for the community. Furthermore, many of the chamber members are small business owners—just like you. They'd love to have you be an economic asset, and they will do anything they can to help your company become successful.

Owning your own business is the ultimate experience in self-reliance, pride, freedom, and the realization of the American Dream. Any American who is even remotely interested in these things should seriously think about starting his own business.

<u>Local Small businesses is a key to our modern economy</u>

Local businesses are the foundation of American prosperity. Many people today incorrectly tend to think of businesses in terms of large businesses and corporations. Whether a person looks for a place to work, or looking for goods and services, many people think in terms of the larger companies. However, it is in fact the smaller businesses that really are the foundation of America.

Look at this from a very personal perspective: Are you laid off? Then get together with a dozen of your colleagues who are also laid off, and start your own company. Tired of the way the corporate world treats you? Then find yourself a smaller, more personal business to work for.

Are the services you want—such as banks and insurance agencies—not caring about you as a customer, or not offering services you expect? Then take your business elsewhere. There is a smaller company with the dedication to service you expect, who started their business just for people like you.

So you see, these small businesses are the key. The free market allows competition. When companies start treating customers poorly, or refusing to offer their services, the local businesses will take them. When you work for another company, you will help that one grow, and take market share away from the big boys. When you start your own company, taking your experience with you (which the corporation didn't appreciate), then you will have the last laugh, as you take market share away from those corporations.

Americans also complain—rightly so—that many good jobs are going overseas. There are many ways to combat this problem, though I cannot expand on them here. However, small local businesses are one way. Remember, you and your buddies have the experience in your field, so you can start your own business. You will be employed, and no one can fire you. You will suffer less from the whims of over-paid executives or from the reading of tea leaves in Wall Street. As a bonus, your potential for income will be unlimited.

Small, local businesses can be anything—restaurants, banks, shipping—even industrial parts and high tech services. Whether you sell directly to the people, or sell to other businesses, there are plenty of needs in your local area. With the experiences of yourself and your colleagues, you can create your own successful, local business.

Further, when communities shop locally the whole community grows. Local businesses help each other thrive. This is one way for individuals to have steady income, and for the entire local economy to be healthy. As a bonus, communities will become stronger and more personal.

Small businesses are at one disadvantage however: advertising. Smaller businesses can't afford major advertising, and it is because they don't have the big ads that you are not aware of these good businesses. You must look around to find them. You must look through chamber of commerce directories, phone books, talking with friends, and driving around. The effort of looking will be well worth it, for you will be much happier as an employee and as a customer.

We must no longer think in terms of the big businesses and big corporations. We must think in terms of small businesses. We must think in terms of companies where the owner is local, and of local businesses who want long term, personal relationships with members of the community.

Hindrance to economic prosperity in America: Government and Socialists

Earlier I said that the pioneering spirit of America is very much alive and well. This is only partially true. The spirit of Americans is very much alive and well. However, there are obstacles put in our way recently which must be eliminated.

The greatest obstacle for Americans to be self-reliant business owners is the government. In recent years, the government has become more and more of an impediment to the prosperity in this country.

All levels of government make laws interfering with the free market system. City councils, state legislatures, and the many agencies of the Federal government all contribute to this problem.

Our various levels of government make more and more regulations for businesses to comply with. Most of these are a nuisance to the business, and yet do not provide any real benefits to the community.

Many legislators view the business world in terms of large corporations. True, there are many of these large businesses. However, there are many more people who work for small businesses or who own their own business than who are involved in a large corporation.

Small businesses cannot handle the burdens imposed by government. For example, a large business can wait patiently for permits, but a small business often can't. Small businesses often do not have the cash on hand to survive until then.

A second example: lawyers are often needed to decipher the many laws. The various governments have created such a patchwork of laws that it is difficult to try to figure out how to run a business by all these laws simultaneously. A large business can hire experts in each of these areas. However, a smaller business has only a few people, and it is often up to the owner to try to meet the legal constraints at the same time that he manages production and sales. This is too cumbersome for a local guy just trying to run an honest business.

For all sizes of businesses, much of their time (too much time) is taken up just by the ongoing task of meeting government regulations. If a company is too small to handle this, they either get beaten up by some regulation they didn't follow, or they go out of business trying to meet the regulation.

Even if a company is large enough to do all of this, the whole process of meeting regulations is expensive. Experts are hired to take care of the details. Fees are paid for various permits. Equipment must be bought just to meet a government specification. All these costs are added into the cost of production, which is then passed on to the consumer.

Thus, when the government over-regulates business, nobody wins. Over-regulation kills small businesses and destroys our economic prosperity.

<u>Hurting the American Spirit</u>

Killing small businesses with regulations is not just bad for our economic prosperity as a whole, but it destroys the American spirit.

Lack of competition is bad for America. I know as absolute fact, from many examples, that a small business *can* beat the big guys. When the American businessman creates a good product that the people really want, then he will take the entire market share from the big boys. It happens again and again and again. Free market means competition, which means better products for everyone.

However, with too many government regulations, small businesses can't compete. The product may be great, but they don't have enough money or time to make the product and at the same time deal with the government bureaucracies. The small business goes under. Hence, we have less competition, and the good products and services that people want are not getting to the people who want them.

More important is that we are not allowing individuals to become self-reliant, wealthy individuals.

We described how anyone can start a business in America. Anyone, even an immigrant who just arrived, can create a successful business. He can become self-reliant, answering to nobody else. That is pure freedom. He can also make himself as wealthy as he wants to be. That is the American dream.

However, if you kill the small businesses, then you kill the American dream.

Why do so many people think that starting their own business just can't be done anymore? Why do we see so many chain stores instead of more local businesses by local entrepreneurs? Government hindrance is one of the primary causes.

<u>One example of over regulation hurting the small business</u>

One recent example in my local area will illustrate the point. A man owned a bakery. His business was so successful, that he wanted to expand. He found an old bakery downtown which was now defunct. This seems like an obvious solution! It is the same type of business, so there should be no zoning problems, right? There should be no modification to the building, right?

Wrong. This man went through a government consigned purgatory as he went through the channels and the paperwork and the fees…. It was over 6 months later that he finally gave up.

His effort to expand his business was almost making him lose his business—and he hadn't even got the approval.

Again, the existing building used to have the exact same type of business that he has. This man was going to hire more people and grow the economy, but he couldn't get through the government process.

This is just one story of hundreds of stories out there. Many hard working entrepreneurs have come up with a good product and sound business management, only to founder due to government regulations. It is true that some businesses will go under because of the free market—bad product, bad management and so forth—but today, the biggest killer of small businesses is government regulation.

<u>Need for government regulations</u>

Some people will argue that some government regulations are necessary. Perhaps some regulations are important. However, I cannot state here which are good and which are not. This is because for each regulation, the relevance is left for the people of each community to decide. Yet, at this point in time, the total of government regulations is such a monstrosity that we must fight to break free. For a while, it would be better for us to err on the side of too few government regulations in business than to have our economy strangled by government regulations.

We must reduce government regulations

Remember we said that the main contrasting economic system to the free market is socialism. We said that socialism is the government taking control of all economics. We also said that socialism always fails.

This is where some people are trying to take us. The government puts more and more restrictions on the way we do business. In the end, their goal is to have government control all aspects of all businesses. We must not let them do this.

We already see businesses having problems due to over-regulation. We've already seen socialist nations become economic disasters. Do we need any more proof? Of course we don't. Too much government regulation, at any and all levels, is dangerously harmful to the economic prosperity of our country.

The situation reminds me of the temples from the Mayan civilization. Over hundreds of years, the jungle took over the area. Only after people hacked and slashed their way through could the beautiful temples be seen. Like that situation, we must slash through the government regulations, take away all the laws that are overgrown, and let the new businesses thrive.

Summary of Free Market Economy

The free market economy is an economic system where the people themselves determine what to make and what to sell. This gives the people better quality goods and services; it gives people the goods they want; and this ensures that there are no shortages of anything.

As much as possible, the government should not be involved with business affairs. Government legislation is more often a hindrance to prosperity than a help, and usually interferes more with an individual's economic success than helping him along.

The economic system in America has two key elements: a free market economy and opportunity for everyone. One of the greatest aspects of this American economic system is that anybody with the right product and with dedication to his vision can create his own highly successful business.

Anyone can Succeed: Opportunity for All

Basic Truth of America #5:
Success in America depends on two things:

a) The Freedoms we have unique to this country
b) An individual's determination and personal sacrifice.

Success in America is *not* determined by a man's economics, his race, or by the government.

<u>Anyone can succeed</u>

In America, anyone can succeed. Our freedoms guarantee that the government will not hinder us. We are allowed to govern ourselves and to make our own choices.

America also guarantees the opportunity for all men and all women. Yet, wealth and happiness are not given to anyone, particularly not by the government. You have the freedom to pursue wealth, yet you must work for it. You have the opportunities to create success, but you alone must create it. You choose how to be happy, for the government will not tell you how to do that.

However, the good news is that this self-government principle allows for an even greater success than if you were dictated to. If you work hard, and if you are creative, then there is no limit on your success. There is no limit on your wealth or on reaching goals. Other countries want to limit your success and limit your wealth. This is not so in America. In America, your success can be as big as your dreams.

Freedoms we have are essential for us to succeed

When this country first started, this was indeed an experiment. No one knew if it would work. Could the people really govern themselves?

In general, the answer is yes. If people have the freedom to make choices, then they will be able to govern their lives, and do so very well.

However, some people will tell you that the answer is no. Aristocrats have long believed that only they, the wealthy landowners and elite, are the wise ones. These aristocrats think that only they, the elite aristocrats, know best how to run the communities. These aristocrats think that the peasants and slaves couldn't possibly know how to run their own lives.

This, of course, is not true. All men and women have the ability, and the right, to make choices and to become successful. The truth is that people anywhere can govern themselves successfully, as long as they are allowed to be free.

Aristocrats had this elitist argument in the feudal system of the middle ages. They had this argument for owning slaves in the 1800s. The liberal elite have this same view today.

This is why our Freedoms are so important. There will always be some aristocratic elites who try to keep the people down. We must always fight them in order to maintain our freedoms.

Would you rather govern yourself, or would you rather be "taken care of" by the aristocrats? The liberal aristocrats will "take care" of you by feeding you a meager diet, but they won't let you flourish. They would let you will exist, but just barely. You will become in essence a slave, or as a prisoner held in a cage.

The liberal elitists are always writing laws to limit the people from living their lives, or to enslave them with meager government handouts. This is not freedom.

In order for all Americans to truly succeed, then every man and every woman must be free. He must be free to govern himself, as he thinks best, for his own life. When each man is allowed to make choices about his own life, then, and only then, can that person become successful.

Without these freedoms, each man is limited. No matter how smart or capable a person is, without freedoms this man is enslaved. Too many people in the government are trying to enslave us; we must always fight them to ensure our personal freedoms. If you truly want wealth and success, then you must fight to be free.

But you must work for it—no one will give it to you

The principle of self-government implies that you can govern yourself.

You are responsible for your own life. You must make your own choices. You must work hard for your goals. You must be responsible for your actions.

If you want a goal, then you must work for it. If you want an education, then you must study. If you want a good job, or advance in your career, then you must work hard at it.

You must also accept responsibility for your actions. If you do not study, then it is your fault for not passing the class or getting into college. If you do not work hard, then it is your fault for not getting the promotion. If you commit a crime, then you must pay the penalty.

This may sound harsh, but it is the reality. In America, you govern your own life. No one will do it for you. The only other contrast—that of not having to make choices—is slavery.

The good news is that because you govern your own life, then you can be happier. You can do what pleases you. You have the freedom to create your own success.

So, self-government is a multifaceted concept. You are free to make choices, but you alone must make them. You are free to pursue success, but you alone must work for it. You are free to take risks and to try new things, but you alone must accept responsibility for bad actions and for failures.

The good news in all this is that anyone can succeed. Self-government gives us the chance to be happy, the chance to be rich, the chance to be successful.

The government does *not* guarantee that you will have these things. What the government *does* guarantee is that you have the freedom to make your own choices, and that you have the opportunity to be successful. You must work yourself to attain this success, yet at the same time your potential for success is unlimited.

Opportunity for all

America gives opportunity to all people. That is unique in the world, for many other countries limit one type of person or another. This is not so in America. Only in America is there equal opportunity for all people.

America gives equal opportunity for men and for women. America gives equal opportunity for all religions. America gives equal opportunity for people of all skin colors.

It doesn't matter what your background is, or what your economic circumstances are, America gives you equal opportunities. It does not even matter what your physical traits are, for your appearance and physical limitations do not deny you equal opportunities.

To repeat: America gives equal opportunities for all people. What, then, are some of these wonderful opportunities?

You have the opportunity to find out what you want to do with your life, and you have the opportunity to make that a reality. You have the opportunity to find what you enjoy—hobbies, career, and lifestyle, and then the freedom to do what you enjoy.

You have the opportunity to better yourself. You can get a college education. You can learn any job skills. You can work as hard as you want to make yourself as rich as you want.

You have the opportunity to start your own business. You have the opportunity to follow your passion and become wealthy at the same time.

You have the opportunity to go to the church of your choice and to express yourself as you want.

You have the opportunity to make anything out of your life that you want. The only thing limiting your success in America is you

<u>But you must seize the opportunities or create your own</u>

There is a catch, however. The catch is that you must seize the opportunity. The opportunity is always there. However, the opportunity isn't coming to you; you have to go for the opportunity.

You have the opportunity of free education through high school, but you have to study. You have the opportunity to go to college, but you have to study hard to get in, and study even harder to get that degree. You have the opportunity to hold a high paying job, but you have to earn the degree and you have to prove your abilities. You have the opportunity to start your own business, but you have to take it in hand and do it.

In America, we offer equal opportunity for all. But that is just an opportunity. You have to take that opportunity, and you have to work for the success that you want.

<u>Everyone has limitations</u>

Too many people today think that they are the only ones with problems. Let's set this straight right now: every person in America has disadvantages.

Everyone has both advantages and disadvantages. The secret is knowing how to use the advantages you have, and working to get beyond the disadvantages placed before you.

Successful people know to make the best of what they have, for nobody has a perfect situation. So, you make the best of what you have today, then you learn what you need, and you work hard in order to move on to something better. That is the American Way.

Summary
Success in America depends on two things: a) The Freedoms we have unique to this country, b) An individual's determination and personal sacrifice. Success in America is *not* determined by a man's economics, his race, or by the government.

Freedoms are essential to success. In order for all Americans to truly succeed, then every man must be free. He must be free to govern himself, as he thinks best, for his own life.

America gives equal opportunity for all. America offers equal opportunity for both sexes, for all religions, and for all races. Only in America do people find such equality.

Anyone can succeed in America. It does not matter how poor you are, where you live, or what your background is. If you have the drive, then you can become successful.

There is a catch—you must work yourself. No one will give success to you. You must work for it. Furthermore, everyone has disadvantages to start. However, successful people work hard and are creative in order to get beyond their disadvantages.

Success can be defined however you want. That is one of our Freedoms in America. You also have opportunity to go after your success. No one is limiting you. That, too, is part of our Freedoms in America. You must work hard for your success, but no one will stop you from becoming successful. That is the American Way.

Freedom, Choice, and Success

Freedom gives us choice. This is a great way to live, for each American is able to make the decision that is right for him.

However, this can also be daunting. With so many choices, sometimes an American can become paralyzed with indecision. What should I do for my career? Where should I go to college? Where should I live? Who will I marry?

Yes, life is full of choices. Although having so many choices can seem confusing, in the end it is much better. Sure, if you had only a few choices, then you wouldn't have to think as much. But would you be as happy? With more options, you can find a choice that is better suited just for you! Thus, although the plethora of choices in America can turn decision making into a more complex process, after you make the decision then you personally will be that much happier.

Choice is an important concept, one that too few people understand. Therefore it is important that I spend some time with the issues involved regarding choice.

Choice means giving up one thing in favor of another

In order to be successful, you must make choices. You will have to give up something.

For example, if you wish to do well in college, then you must study. This means that you cannot party with your friends as much as you want. You must choose that your education is more important to you than going out.

Another example is paying for college. You may not be rich enough to afford college straight out, so you choose to work your way through. You choose to take a job and accept the extra work because you want the education.

Even successful artists had to make choices. Many of them didn't do anything else in their early years but practice and perform. While their friends just relaxed during summers and on the weekends, these musicians and actors drove many miles to perform at any small venue they could find. They made a choice to sacrifice all their time early in their lives in order to achieve a larger goal.

Moving is also common. Your ideal job may not be in this city, so you may have to move far away. Which is more important to you—your ideal job in a new city, or staying close to your friends and family? That is a choice you must make. One choice is not better than another, only what is right for you. Yet it is a choice, and you must give up something.

We must also understand that there is not always a "right" answer to these personal choices. Whatever choice you make, you will have gained one thing, and given up another.

A personal example

I will offer a personal example. I had to choose between a wonderful new job and a wonderful new girl.

I had wanted to develop a new career. As I worked my current job I learned more about another career which interested me more, and so I decided (another choice) to take my life in that direction. I worked hard and finally got a job offer, but it was in another state several hundred miles away.

The problem was that I was dating a girl. I really liked this girl—she had potential.

A wonderful job or a wonderful girl—both here at the same time. That was the choice to make, and it was a difficult choice. I made a sacrifice. I turned down the wonderful job and the career I really wanted, and instead took a chance that this girl might be worthwhile. This was a tough choice, and there were no guarantees.

I ended up marrying the girl, and we've been happily married for many years.

I chose. I gave up the career to try for the girl. Although the girl was no guarantee, I took the chance. My life would have been very different had I gone after that career, but I would not change things because I am very happy with the girl who is now my wife.

Thus it is with all choices—you must sacrifice one thing in order to gain something else that is of greater value to you. This also shows that you must also take risks, for very few things in life are guarantees.

Owning your mistakes, your bad choices, and your failures

Another misunderstood concept regarding choices is owning your mistakes. Failures are yours. If you work hard at a goal but fail, that failure is yours. This is not a bad thing, just own it. You learn from this failure, and you will do better the next time.

Many successful businessmen failed the first few times before their great success. All great actors have been in a flop at least once in their lives. Many great political leaders have lost elections once before winning the next time, and many generals have lost a battle before winning the war. Failure is not bad if you own it and if you learn from it. You made the choice, then you saw the results. Next time your choice will be much wiser.

If you make poor choices then those choices are yours as well. If you choose to take drugs, to commit a crime, or to be lazy, then the consequences are yours. You cannot blame anyone but yourself for the life you have created.

You made poor choices in life. Just own it, admit to it, and learn from it. You may not have many good things in your life at this point, but you still have freedom of choice. You can always choose to better your situation. The question is, will you do it?

Second Chances

America is the land of second chances. Failed at your business? Start another. Didn't finish school? Take night classes. In America, we can fail two, three, even ten times, and still get back up again. There is nothing stopping you from trying again.

In America, you can change your path: Change jobs. Change careers. Get a new education. Move to a different city. Build a new house. Start a new business. There is nothing preventing you from changing directions anywhere along your path.

Some pessimistic people will find excuses—no money, no time, no opportunities. Fight those thoughts. Where there is a will, there is a way.

No money is your excuse? Get a loan, take a second job, or move to a cheaper neighborhood.

No Time? Make time. All of us have 24 hours in a day; successful people are not given any more. If you want something strongly enough, then you can figure out how to make the time for it.

No opportunities? You may have to create opportunities. Many people find opportunities by starting with a smaller company or moving to a different town. Other people create opportunities by starting their own company.

This is America—you almost always have a second chance. If you failed at one thing or made poor choices, you can always start again. If you don't like a choice you made, or don't like the path you are on, you can always change.

Sometimes you've got to look carefully to find the second chance, and sometimes you've got to create it, but in America there is almost always a second chance to be had. Most importantly, however, is that you've got to act on that second chance. No one will do it for you.

Guidance in making choices

This leads us to the concepts of guidance and wisdom. With so many choices, why not ask for guidance? You can get guidance everywhere. You can find authors who have written books on every subject. Many experts are willing to counsel you for a fee. Friends and family are wonderful sources of advice. Many Americans rely on God for guidance.

Perhaps the best untapped source of guidance is from elders in your community. With age comes experience, and with experience comes wisdom. Ask the experienced and wise elders in your community for guidance. They often know more than you think.

We have lost this concept today and need to regain it. The wise elders, such as teachers, parents, grandparents, industry leaders, and retired Americans have much wisdom to give. They have made more choices than you can imagine, and they have learned more than you probably realize.

Ask for guidance and learn from anyone you can. The final choices are yours and yours alone, but it is a good idea to ask for guidance along the way.

Summary

Yes, life is full of choices. The freedom we have in this country allows us to choose our paths for ourselves. Self-government means that we can run our own lives.

We have numerous choices. To some people this is frightening because choices make life confusing and because they don't want to be responsible for their choices. However, most Americans will agree that having choice is a blessing.

Freedom of choice is a blessing because these choices are ours to make, and the choices we make usually lead to a better life. Even when a particular choice leads you to a mistake, you are now wiser, and are able to make better choices in the future. At the very least, your mistakes can be lessons that can guide the next generation. Your bad choices will never be a complete waste—unless you fail to learn from them.

Choice allows us greater success and greater happiness than if we lived in a society with limited choices. We must own our mistakes and our failures; from these we learn and chose more wisely in the future. Freedom of choice is complex, but it is a wonderful American principle.

Government, Taxes, and Budgets

The relationships between the American people and the levels of government regarding financial issues are very important. America has its own culture in these areas.

Principles regarding money, taxes, government, and the people

1. Income is created by the citizens. No government can ever create wealth.

2. All money spent by the government comes from the people.

3. The government treasuries belong to the people, not to those who work for the government.

4. The people must have the greatest control over money.

5. Limited government is always the best government.

6. The people can govern their own lives, and can do so better than any government agency ever could.

7. Solutions are always more effective and cost less when we use personal control and local control rather than state or federal agencies.

8. The people need government only when absolutely necessary.

9. Government is necessary only when a) the solution is more effectively operated through the community as a whole rather than by individuals, and b) the need is funded better by all the people for the community rather than by each individual for his own need.

10. To fund these community needs, the cost is spread among all the people of the community, and each member pays his share of the cost through taxes.

11. We hire representatives as our agents to administer our public money for the public good. Although we give these representatives certain authority, they work for us. The money belongs to the people, not to the representatives.

12. Because the representatives are merely agents who work for the people, then the people have a right to investigate all government expenses. We have a right to see how every dollar is spent, at any time we choose.

13. If our agents (representatives) are not good managers of the public money, then we must replace them in the next election.

14. Representatives, at every level, must always work for the following: a) give more control to the people, b) give more control to local areas, c) trim down the size of the government agencies, d) reduce the scope of government's authority, e) reduce government spending, and f) lower all taxes.

Any representative which does not work for these goals or who does not believe in these goals must be replaced immediately. This representative is not capable of managing our money.

Control over money—the hierarchy

1. Individual citizens

The people have the greatest control over their money and how money is spent.

2. Community groups and neighborhoods

The people themselves volunteer their own time and their own money through these community groups to make effective improvements in their own communities.

These include formal groups such as Rotary Club, Boy Scouts, and Chamber of Commerce, as well as semi-formal groups such as neighborhood associations, crime watch groups, and church groups.

Note that if the federal government and state government tax the people less, then the people will have more money for community groups.

3. City and County government
Local government is best. Furthermore, the items that most Americans use from any government is local, such as fire, police, EMS, schools, city parks, and sanitation services.

Note that if the federal government and state government tax the people less, then there will be more money available for city taxes. The money is best spent here since the most benefits for the public are city and county services.

4. State government
The few items larger than the local cities and counties are left up to the state. State government is as large as most government involvement and expenses should really be.

5. Federal government
The Federal government should have the least control over how the people's money is spent. The federal government should pay for only those items necessary to the national good.

Government Budgets

Representatives are merely agents we hire

Remember that our representatives in legislatures are merely agents who work for us. This is much like when we hire a business manager—we may have authorized him to run the finances, but it still our money, and we get several rights with this:
1. It is our right to see every expense.
2. It is our right to see the books at any time we desire.
3. It is our right to pay for what we want.
4. It is our right to not pay for what we don't want.

We may technically have representation, but in actual practice, it seems nothing of the sort. The government taxes the people to pay for programs, taking money from people who worked hard for it, and we are not even consulted in the process.

Further, if we refuse to pay our taxes? We get fined excessive amounts or thrown in jail. Representation? More like extortion.

Therefore it is important, as well as our absolute right, to see the budget of every legislature of our area: city, state, and federal.

We should see the budget

We the people must know what the budget is for our Federal, State, and City governments. Sadly, many governments keep the budget hidden. Even when you go to the sites of the budget office, the budget you get is very, very skimpy—it does not mention many of the items we know the government spends money on.

What the people need and what the people must clamor for is a proper detailed budget.

We need to know where our money is going—down to the penny. Only then will we be able to have an intelligent discussion about government spending.

This is what we should call for, what the government should do for its people regarding budgets:

1. Have a full, detailed budget—every item, down to the penny—available on a website.

Note that this can't be just a PDF file we have to download just to see it either. (Many budgets offered today are merely PDF, which is unrealistic). This must be an easy to access website, where we can click the links and jump ahead to any page of the budget.

A detailed budget accessible on-line must be available for the Federal budget, for every state budget, and for city budgets of larger cities.

2. One printed copy of the detailed budget should be put on CD-ROM and distributed to a public library per population of residents.

For the Federal budget this CD-ROM should be sent to a library per 500,000 residents. For the state budget, this CD-ROM should be sent to a library per 100,000 residents. For the city budget, a copy of the annual budget should be placed in the central library of every city.

3. <u>A 25–100 page summary of the budget should be distributed to every home, every year.</u>

This is much like stockholders who get an annual report or employees who get annual booklets on updated benefit information. Each American pays into the government, and so each household has a right to have an annual update of how their money is being spent.

100 pages aren't that much. A typical monthly magazine runs 100 pages or more, and they publish every month. Surely the Federal government could print up a 100 page summary of the budget once a year.

The Federal government should create a 100–150 page summary of the budget, and distribute it to every household.

The state government should create a 50–100 page summary of the budget and distribute it to every household.

The summaries put out by cities will vary according to their size. Larger cities have more complex responsibilities, and therefore their summary must be larger.

Some guidelines: Cities and metro areas with a population of 1 million or more should have a 50—75 page summary. Cities with a population of 500,000 to 1 million should make a 25–50 page summary. Cities with a population of 50,000 to 500,000 should have a 10–25 page summary. Lesser populations can distribute what they can afford; even a 1 page annual report sent to all residents of a small village will be helpful to the citizens.

<u>Creating the websites</u>

The websites will be the most useful for citizens to see how their money is spent. Websites are relatively cheap to run, even for large entities such as state and federal governments. The budget can be easily accessed by all citizens. Even those without computers will be able to access the budget web sites from the computers at public libraries.

Further, since the budget in full will be lengthy and complex, it is easier to read on a website. The nature of websites makes jumping through pages easy. A contents page in the front will link the category of the budget to the appropriate section.

We need to have a combination of creators for the website. The layout must be logical for the average citizen, so an average but organized citizen must help in the design. In the design, the citizen user must be able to find the expense topic he is interested in, and jump right there.

Yet also, the entire budget, in detail, must be there. This will be the place for detailed data. Those who work in the budget office will ensure all the facts are on the site. However, other people must be involved so that the categories and terms make sense to the average citizen.

At the end of each section, there should be a contact for more information. For example, when a citizen sees expenses for grants to scientific studies, and wants to know more details on what studies were given money, he should have an easy way of contacting the office who approved those grants for more detailed information.

This could further be made easier, by each government organization having its own web page with its own budget. One click from the main government page on grants to scientists goes right to the budget from that department. The citizen can then see the details of what grants were given, and to whom. No government employee needs to be bothered.

Because so many people will be accessing this site, there should be a server dedicated just to the budget.

Old budgets can be stored on a computer permanently. Citizens should be able to access old budgets for many reasons, including historical studies and noting trends. Each budget office can decide best how to do this. One way would be to store old budgets on a separate computer. Citizens who wish to see these budgets could purchase them, and have them shipped on CD-ROM.

Writing the summaries that are mailed to the homes

It is very important that the government make sure that the summary budgets are well written. We should have a combination of writers, teachers, accountants, and graphic designers to create these summaries.

The goal is to be accurate, but make it easy for the people to understand. There will be data, tables, and graphs, but these have to make sense to the people. There will be terms, but these words must be words that the people understand, not government jargon.

Cost of these websites and the summaries

I am sure that some people will argue that this will cost money. I have several answers to this. Having these budgets are so important that I must spend time explaining good reasons for the cost.

First, the governments, particularly state and federal, spend billions and trillions of dollars. Most of these items are not necessary. The cost of giving the people disclosure of the budget is very small compared to the cost of many programs which the people do not want to pay for.

Secondly, it is our right. We are in charge, they are the employees. We earned the money, they are merely the agents. Therefore, we have every right to see where our money is going. All smart businessmen do this—all good businessmen look at the spending of their departments. Looking at the details of the expenses makes for good business, and it makes wise stewardship of the public funds.

Third, the government spends lots of money on many things the people don't approve of. This happens in business as well, such as when a man buys himself a fancy car or expensive lunches, all at the owner's expense. The people, too, must watch what the government spends. If we do not watch them, then the government will waste our money.

Finally, the government is always telling the people that they need more money. But, do they really need it?

The people know how to live on a budget. They cannot just ask their employer for more, nor can we just take it from our neighbor. We know how to adjust our lives, such as staying in a Motel 6 rather than a five star hotel, or eating at Denny's instead of a steak restaurant. Yet, we can still stay a motel, and take our family to dinner.

The same holds for the government—there are always areas to reduce spending and get the same results. Furthermore, to repeat an important concept, in many cases, the government spends money on items we don't want them to pay for.

The creation of these accessible budgets will allow all citizens to really see what we are paying for. Then, just as in a family budget, we can discuss the priorities, cut out what we don't need, and find ways to economize.

Therefore, the small expenses involved in creating these accessible budgets will save us, the taxpayers a lot of money. Taxes will remain low, and the governments will rarely be in debt again.

Summary on budgets

Remember, the money in the government treasuries belongs to the people. The government workers are merely authorized to use the public money for the public good. It is OUR money, not theirs.

The various governments keep this money hidden. They hide it from the people intentionally, for many reasons. We cannot allow this.

When the government spends money without telling the people how they spent it, that is stealing. When the government demands more money without fully explaining why, then that too, is stealing.

We need to write and call our representatives and the budget office. We need full disclosure of where our money is going—and this must be done every year.

Tax issues: further suggestions:

A. If our representatives say they need more money, or if they demand an increase in spending, we have the right to 1) demand to see the budget, 2) and ask what they have done to reduce spending.

B. Many current laws in the United States say that the legislatures may raise taxes and that the people must pay. The law should be changed to where any tax increase or spending increase must be voted on directly by the people.

With such laws, the representatives will truly have to explain to the people why government cannot be trimmed more. More importantly, the money is ours, and if we do not see a need for the extra expense, we must be able to say so.

Wise business owners know to watch their contractors and department managers. These contractors and department managers must *ask* the owner for increases in spending. The owner is then able to say yes or no. We need to have that same ability with government spending.

Summary of Government, Taxes, and Budgets

The people create the wealth. The people are entitled to as much money as they can earn. Government cannot create wealth; it can only take some money from the people and use it for the public good.

Limited government is always best. For almost all areas of life, an individual person can make better choices for himself than any government agency. People must retain the most control over their lives, and the most amount of money that they earn.

A small percentage of each American's money is used for the public good. As a nation of self-government, the people must share in the cost of meeting the needs of the community. However, local government is the best, and government at all levels should be limited in scope.

The money in the public treasuries belongs to the people. Our representatives are merely agents who handle the public business. We hire these agents, and it is our money. These agents (representatives) must tell us fully and openly about all their expenses. If we do not approve of the way they handle our money, then we replace them in the next election.

Citizens must have full detailed budgets accessible to them. Websites are the best tool for this. All legislatures should post their budget on a website each year for all citizens to see how their money is being spent. Only then can the people have an intelligent dialogue about where our money should be best used and on how to trim the budgets.

A good representative must always seek to: give more control to the people, give more control to local governments, reduce government spending, and lower taxes. Any representative who does not do these things should be replaced in the next election.

We do not steal to become successful

Americans do not steal or cheat to become successful. This is not the American Way.

Stealing is fundamentally wrong. It is an ethical code as old as man. The Eighth Commandment reads "You shall not steal." Even wild animals know this—when one animal tries to steal food from another, the rightful owner will fight for his food.

Remember, in America anyone can be successful. You do not have to steal from others to become successful. You can do it yourself. You can have that money and successful life, there is nothing stopping you but yourself.

Teaching that theft is wrong, and stopping theft

Whenever we teach that stealing is wrong, we always use the same concept: Reverse the situation. What if you worked very hard for that money, and then someone just took it away? How would that make you feel?

For many people, once this is explained clearly for the particular situation, then these thieves think differently. Many times, the person does not realize that his action is theft. Thus, when we explain the situation clearly, most of these thieves realize their actions were wrong, and won't do it again.

However, there are many people today who know it is morally wrong, but don't care. These people see theft as the easy way to get what they want. If we were unable to prevent their theft through moral reasoning, then we have no other course than to punish them for their act.

Unfortunately, today many thieves go unpunished. Individuals steal from businesses, managers steal from investors, and the government steals from the people.

People steal yet are not punished. Their stealing is in the open, and fully legal. Government agencies and juries not only allow this theft, but encourage it. They say to the thieves: "That's okay, take it, and here, have some more."

I like the term Jefferson used—"self-evident." That many actions people do are stealing is self-evident. The obviousness of it is so clear, honest people are baffled at how others could see things otherwise. And yet, this is the situation that exists today.

That is why I must devote an entire chapter to the concept that the American Way does *not* include stealing in order to become successful.

<u>Specific acts of stealing in society today</u>

People must be told their behavior is wrong. I have seen this many times as a teacher: a person did not know his behavior is wrong or understand why it is wrong. Therefore, we must explain it. Here, then, is a list of specific acts of stealing which we have seen all too often in our modern society. These acts are not acceptable. We must prevent these from happening, and punish those who do.

1. Downloading music off the computer without paying for it is stealing.

2. Taking money from the government when you are physically able to work is stealing.

3. Demanding services from the government when you are not a citizen is stealing.

4. Billing customers for work you did not do, or not fulfilling your part of the contract is stealing.

6. Increasing government spending at a rate beyond the increase in pay of the average person is stealing.

7. Government spending on frivolous projects is stealing.

8. Taking grants from government for frivolous studies or obscene art is stealing.

9. Suing a business for your error, your stupidity, or a choice you made is stealing.

10. A government that increases taxes when the economy is slow is stealing.

11. Government officials getting a retirement salary using taxpayers money, before the age of 65, is stealing.

12. Redistribution of wealth is stealing.

Further note, as with students, if the person continues in this behavior, then he must be punished. We hope that after being punished a few times, he will stop this stealing.

Note that this is not an exhaustive list. This is only a list of common forms of theft which are not viewed as theft by too many people today.

A few of the more significant items of these will be discussed in more detail.

Trial Lawyers—suing hard working people is stealing

Most lawyers who sue do it not for justice, but for money. They get a large percentage of the awards. Hence, the larger the dollar amount of the reward, the wealthier the lawyers become.

Non-economic damages

Lawyers have long tacked on non-economic damages (pain and suffering) to true economic damages. These damages can be excessive. Why the big sums? The trial lawyers get a nice percentage.

The good news on this one is that many states are proposing laws, or have passed laws, that limit how much a lawyer can ask for in non-economic damages.

Frivolous lawsuits

Many lawsuits are frivolous. Many times an individual does something stupid with a product and then blames the manufacturer. Many times an individual is doing something illegal on another's property, hurts himself, and then blames the property owner for his injury.

Lawyers take on these cases because they *do* win. Juries *do* award the stupid people enormous sums.

We must combat this, on two fronts. First, we must have laws which limit lawsuits based on stupidity. These can be limiting either by how much of an award they can get, or, by limiting what can be heard in court to begin with.

Second, we must educate more people on basic financial matters and business costs. That means we must educate more potential jurors of the consequences of their decisions. We must educate more people that to award money to these so-called victims is actually a form of legalized theft.

Cost of lawsuits on consumers, producers, and society

There are too many people today who think that it is okay to sue someone or some company for money, when the individual was clearly at fault himself. Here are some of the ramifications of awarding money to these thieves.

1. Products cost more because of lawsuits.

The result of that lawsuit cost the company money. That cost is passed on to the consumer.

2. Products cost more, to *prevent* lawsuits.

In order to defend itself and prevent future lawsuits, the company hires lawyers, and changes packaging. That cost is passed on to the consumer.

3. Companies go out of business, people lose jobs.

The company can't afford to keep in business with potential lawsuits, and so they must close down. Many people lose jobs. The entire local economy is affected.

4. Higher doctor fees.

Doctors pay malpractice insurance. The more fraudulent claims against doctors, the higher the fees they must pay. The doctors quit or pass the cost to the patients.

5. Many businesses are small businesses and hurt easily.

Most businesses in America are smaller, yet thieves sue those as well. Small businesses don't have the time to do all the prep work for court and still run their business. The owners aren't trained in law, nor can they afford to hire a good lawyer. The result of many lawsuits, then, is in favor of the criminal, not the hardworking businessman. This is nothing but theft.

6. Lawsuits hurt the American spirit.

In the end, lawsuits hurt the American spirit, because America is no longer the land of opportunity.

Thieves steal from hard working Americans. Hard working Americans get punished for their success. Thus, the American characteristics of hard-work and self-reliance are punished instead of rewarded. This further hurts America as people watch these events: fewer people work for success, and more people steal to get it. This is not the American Way.

These are just a few of the social costs of bad lawsuits and reasons why these lawsuits are nothing but theft. We cannot allow these to continue.

Many states are proposing laws which limit these lawsuits and the awards given. It is important you support these laws.

Furthermore, there are good organizations working on this type of tort reform. These are listed in the Appendix. We must also support those organizations.

Redistribution of Wealth is Stealing—details

Redistribution of wealth is stealing. Receiving entitlements from the government is stealing. It is that simple.

Redistribution of wealth is a socialist idea, and an idea which does not work. Redistribution of wealth is *not* the American Way.

It is wrong to give away the people's money. That is stealing. Yet the socialists push to give money away. They give it away to different groups, always claiming that each group needs it, and that they can't survive without it. Yet, the rest of us managed to get what we needed through hard labor. In America, anyone can earn money through hard work. There is no need to take money from others.

Furthermore, we who work hard for our success experience the government taking our money and giving it to someone who didn't work for it. This is nothing more than legalized theft.

It may be noble to give money to others. But if the "government" gives money, where does this money come from? It comes from the people—the people who work hard to earn their money. This money is taken from them, in effect at gunpoint, as they are forced to pay through higher taxes. The government, of the people, by the people, is stealing from the people.

If you want to give money to someone, then give it from your own pocket. Do not force someone else to give.

Remember, the money in the government does not belong to the representatives. They did not earn it. They took it through taxes. It is the people's money, and the people must be able to decide how the money is spent.

Taking money from the government is really stealing from your neighbors.

It is also wrong as an individual to *take* money from the government. Anything you want in life, you can get if you work for it. If you are physically able, there is no reason why you have to rely on the government to succeed. Education, housing, clothes, medications—all these things you can afford if you work for it. The majority of other Americans did just that.

And again, if you take money from the "government" you are really taking money from your neighbors. Your neighbors paid taxes—a large amount of their paycheck—to the government. Their taxes are higher because people like you are demanding money without working for it. The people would much rather have more of their own money than to give it to you.

On beggars and the budget

This also greatly affects the government budget. The governments, at all levels, constantly talk of being in debt. The governments at all levels talk about needing more money. Well, they wouldn't need more money if they didn't spend money in wrong ways. One of the wrong ways to spend public money is to give it to beggars holding their hands out.

If I personally want to give money to a beggar on the street, I will. If I personally want to donate to a charity, then I will. The government should not be giving to beggars.

These beggars just demand more and more without working for it. Furthermore, as more beggars see that free money is being given out, soon the line of beggars grows to large numbers. Both of these facts make the spending to beggars increase to large proportions. Hence, reduce the giving to these beggars, stop giving out money to those who don't deserve it, and the government budgets will not be in debt and not require so much more money.

Private Charity

Private charity is the best. In this ideal scenario—that is private charity—these citizens are giving their money voluntarily. Voluntary is the key. Giving money voluntarily is ethical, and in fact is the right thing to do in many cases. However, forcing someone to give is immoral.

Furthermore, these citizens can choose who to give money to, and which organizations to support. This is better than the government giving the people's money to people and organizations the people may not want to support.

Finally, these citizens can decide how much to give. They can give more when they have more to give. They will be allowed to hold back giving when they have their own needs to meet.

Americans are generous people. They *do* care. Yet Americans would rather be able to choose where and when to give, and not have it forced from them. The government must not force people to give their money away to other people.

<u>Summary of redistribution of wealth</u>

Again, redistribution of wealth is stealing. Taking entitlements is stealing. It is that simple. Governments have no right to redistribute wealth, and no person has the right to demand entitlements.

Summary of chapter—stealing is not the American Way

Stealing is fundamentally wrong. Even animals know this.

America is a trusting nation. We are honorable people, who deal fairly and honestly with others. This is not so in other countries. I have traveled plenty around the world, and I have seen that honesty and trust are not part of the culture of many places. The people of many countries are dishonest as a way of life. You learn not to trust anyone but yourself in these countries. America is unique in this culture of trust and honesty—and this characteristic is a major reason that we are successful.

It is due to our trust and honesty that we can be more prosperous. It is due to trust and honesty that we have healthier communities, successful businesses, and more satisfied individuals.

In recent times, America has gone away from this. Americans are not only allowed to steal, but are rewarded for it. Immigrants come from these other countries where honesty is not part of their culture—and hence they feel it is their right to steal from Americans. These acts have taken our country in a downward cycle. Businesses stagnate, crime increases, and social problems abound.

There will always be people who think stealing is the best way to get what they want. Whatever form of their theft, we must put a stop to it. Only through education, legislation, and real punishments, will we be able to stop these thieves.

PART V
Being a Good American

Melting Pot and Becoming a Good American

<u>Basic truths of America #3 and #4:</u>

3. There is a distinct American culture.

We are a nation founded on ideals, a vision based upon morals. We have a system of laws and justice, with checks and balances, and administered by the people. Honesty, trust, courtesy, and compassion *do* matter. These are integral parts of the American fabric. We are the true Land of Brotherhood, because Americans know that we must have consideration, kindness, and positive relationships with our neighbors.

4. Out of Many, One

My ancestors may have come from a dozen nations, but I am 100% American.

<u>If you live in America then you must live the American Way</u>

Whether you were born here or came here from another country, if you choose to live in the United States you must live by the American Way. There is no variation on this point.

America allows many lifestyles, yet these must fit into the basic lifestyle of the American Way. The range of acceptable lifestyles is very broad. In fact, no other country in the world allows as many lifestyles as America. However, there are limits.

The American Way includes everything described in this book. That is why I wrote the book—to state clearly what the American way is, and what it is not.

Melting Pot; Out of Many—One

America works because immigrants who come to America adopt America's principles and cultures.

We have the concept known as the melting pot. People from all cultures and from all countries come to America. They assimilate into America by adopting the American Way. Those things that are not necessarily part of the American Way can be left up to the individuals. It is in this way that America preserves its culture, and yet, at the same time, gains contributions from different people.

For hundreds of years immigrants would come to this country and assimilate into America. They would learn English. They would send their children to the schools—free and open to all people. Many of these immigrants prospered much better here than they ever could back in their original country. These immigrants and their descendents would always be proud to call themselves American.

Our coins read "E Pluribus Unum." This phrase means "From Many—One." From many states, we have one nation. From many cultures, we have one culture. From many peoples we have one people.

Americans have chosen to marry people equal to themselves (as all Americans are equal), but of different backgrounds. There are no "pure" races anymore. Ethnicity in America is a delightful blend of everything, mixed and mixed until all the boundaries have long disappeared. There is only one ethnicity in America today: we call it "American."

"American" is a heritage

When you are an American, you take part in the stream of American history and culture. When you are an American, you are joining those who value the American heritage.

"American" is a heritage. Just as those people who proudly call themselves Chinese, Mexican, German, Italian, and so forth are each linking with a particular heritage, so it is when you become an American.

"American" is a culture. "American" is an ethnicity. "American" is a heritage.

Yet, America is unique because we are the only nation to found itself entirely on ideas. Our heritage is defined by philosophical principles, on moral codes, and on behavior. Our heritage is not defined by race, lineage, or geography, as is the case for much of the world. Our definition of heritage makes the United States unique.

Thus, the American heritage—that is, the American Way—must be preserved. All people are welcome to join us, yet you are obligated to accept American principles. If you do join us, then you must assimilate into American society. You must support the American Way and preserve our heritage.

<u>No room for hyphenated Americans in this country</u>

There is no room for hyphenated Americans in this country. You are either an American, or you're not. If you were born here, you are an American. If you are a citizen, you are an American.

If you were born here, then you cannot be African-American, Asian-American, or Hispanic-American. You are American. Only someone born in Africa can say anything about Africa regarding who he is. The same is true for any other group.

All of us, at one point in our family history, came here from a different country. So, in one sense, each of us could call ourselves "German-American", "Irish-Americans", "Italian-Americans" and so forth. Yet this is not only cumbersome, it is ridiculous. America was never about dividing itself into groups, but rather by being an American first and foremost.

Furthermore, due to such marrying of other Americans over hundreds of years, ethnicity is entirely meaningless. If we were to really state our ethnicity in hyphenated form, it would look something like this: "I am an Irish-Italian-German-Cherokee-Chinese American." This is both cumbersome and ridiculous. In reality, we are all "mixed race." We are all Americans.

More importantly, the very nature of America is a principle of community and equality. When various groups of people separate themselves they divide the community. These groups force people to notice their differences rather than notice the commonalities.

Dividing cultures also makes people unequal. In America, all people are viewed equally with regard to freedoms and the law. However, when groups of people, such as many of the black culture, divide themselves and want special advantages, then they are no longer viewed as equal. They demand special privileges for themselves, and demand additional focus on themselves. This is unequal. Furthermore, these advantages are often advantages which most Americans do not get. Therefore, hyphenated Americans are violating the prime American principle of equal opportunity for all.

Thus, hyphenated Americans have no place in our society. The very nature of calling yourself other than "American" makes you not an American. Groups such as the so called "African-Americans" actually harm themselves by dividing themselves from the rest of America, and by demanding favorable treatment. (This is further made clear by the demands that hyphenated Americans make for themselves). This is a very un-American concept, and must be eliminated.

You cannot change the American Way

Everyone who lives here must adopt the American Way. The American Way includes: the Constitution, principle of self-government, equality, ethics, community spirit, and a positive attitude.

You may not like some of the American Way, but you cannot change it. If an American goes to another country, would he be able to change the laws and culture? No. Nobody in that country would seriously listen to a foreigner who wants to make changes in a foreign country. Each country has its own culture and laws; visitors either adapt to them or go home. This holds for any visitors to any nation.

The same hold true for America. America has its own laws and culture. Why should we change? America has a distinct culture—a culture which the great majority of Americans love. If an immigrant finds America so distasteful, then he should leave. (For that matter, so should liberals who hate America—they can leave, too).

Do not try to change the American Way just because you don't like it. Agree with the American Way, or do not live in America. It is that simple.

English

English is the national language in America. Everyone must learn to speak English, and learn to speak it properly.

The purpose of language is communication. We must have a common language if we are to communicate with each other. America has immigrants from many nations, so we must have an official language. All immigrants must learn this one language so that everyone can live together and so that all the citizens can govern their communities. Therefore, it is essential that everyone who lives and works in America learns to speak English.

Immigrants must learn to speak English. We do not have to have our government cater to those who speak other languages. Businesses *can* cater to immigrants who are not yet proficient in English—that is the right of those businesses, and that can be good for them. Yet, we should not print public documents, signs, or hold public discussions in any other language but English. All immigrants must learn English.

English must also be spoken properly. It is true that there are regional accents, and difference in phrases. However, most Americans still speak English in a way which is understood.

The main contrasting subculture in this area is the black culture. The language they speak is not remotely related to English. I know—I've taught at inner city schools for many years. The black culture prides itself on speaking this truly foreign language, and yet at the same time, they wonder why they don't get hired for the best jobs. These black people must learn to speak English properly in order to function as Americans. There is no second option here.

Summary

America has a unique culture, collectively known as The American Way. Anyone who lives here must adopt the American Way, the details of which are described in this book.

"American" is a heritage. It is a culture, and it is an ethnicity. All people who are born in America have the same ethnic background: "American."

All who enjoy America's freedoms and blessings must call themselves "American." All who live here must adopt the ways of America, become members of the communities, and preserve the American heritage.

Good Neighbors and Community Spirit

The American Way includes being a good neighbor. Furthermore, American principles are merely concepts until Americans bring them to life. Therefore, having good relationships with all your neighbors and being actively involved with your community are absolute essentials to living the American Way.

Americans have long had a strong sense of community. By necessity, Americans have had to work together as they created each new town and settled each new territory. Community spirit and being a good neighbor have been part of our American heritage.

In recent years, communities have fallen to personal islands. Many reasons can explain this. However, there is no need to despair, for there are many neighborhoods that still have a strong community spirit. They may be more difficult to find, and they are too few in number, but these communities are alive and well.

Furthermore, anyone can create the good neighborhoods we yearn for. The solutions are so simple that anyone can make them into a reality.

The simplest actions are often the best. It is not necessary to have a large neighborhood project or a formal group to have a good neighborhood. Simple acts of kindness in the daily lives of our neighbors often make the most impact.

It is important to remember that good neighborhoods do not just happen. We have to make them happen. A neighborhood is not just buildings which are physically close to each other, but rather people who are emotionally close to each other. If you want a quality neighborhood, you must first be a good neighbor yourself.

Sphere of influence

Each man has a sphere of influence. This includes his friends, his family, his co-workers, and his neighbors. How he interacts with each person is very important.

Each man must look for the opportunity to improve his sphere of influence. Each man has the obligation to be moral, to be humane, and to use his power to truly make his world a bit better, piece by piece, and day by day.

In other words, a man must take an interest in people while pursuing his professional goals. A man must be a Guardian of values in his neighborhood while pursuing his personal pleasures. He must be an active citizen of his city while becoming financially successful.

Smiles, Courtesy

The first level of civics in the community is being friendly and courteous. Be a courteous and polite driver on your way to work. Say hello to co-workers. Hold a door open for strangers. Smile when you're at the delicatessen. Chat with the cashier.

Always try to be friendly and courteous. These small acts actually make people feel just a bit better. Not only will you have touched them, but they in turn will be a bit more courteous with others. Smile, be courteous, and pass it on.

Meeting new neighbors

The best place to start for being a good neighbor is meeting the people who move into your neighborhood.

While they are still unloading their truck, go over and introduce yourself. Better yet, help them unload. Moving is a laborious task, and if you help them, even for just an hour, the new neighbors will never forget it. Make lunch for them and bring some drinks. Your new neighbors will undoubtedly be hungry and will be working up a thirst.

When they've just moved in, bring a housewarming gift, such as a small plant, a dessert, or a helpful list of the best local stores. Invite their whole family for dinner, and set a specific date so it really happens.

Make your new neighbors feel welcome from the very first. You will have won their hearts from the beginning, and have started on your way to a solid friendship.

Helping neighbors when they are sick or on vacation

A good neighbor helps others in time of need. When a neighbor is ill, then you should bring food, watch the children, or run some errands for him. A good neighbor will also help another during difficult times, listening and being supportive as best he can. When a neighbor is on vacation, another good neighbor will watch the house for thieves, and even take care of the pets.

Be a friend

Offer unconditional friendship to others. Approach those who seem especially to need a friend. There will always be snobs who might not associate with a person because of his looks or his job, but you see right past that. You see a person. You see an untapped source of wisdom, an untapped source of fun times, and a potential friendship for you to enjoy. Be a friend, unconditionally.

When you look at people, don't think "what can they do for me." Instead, think "what can I do for them." This thought has a great difference in relationships. The impact it has can be quite profound.

If you look for ways to help another person, you can usually find one. Sometimes people don't even know what they need or know how to ask for help. When you see a need that others don't, that is the time to suggest it to them. When you can offer something that another is afraid to ask for, then it is time to offer yourself to them. Not only is it the right thing to do, it also makes you feel good.

When you offer unconditional help and when you offer unconditional friendship, you create the truest form of friendships.

Mentor a youth

Young people always need guidance. Parents and teachers offer the most guidance. However a young person often needs more. Young people need guidance and friendship from adults who are not their parents. When you are in the right place to mentor, do so unequivocally.

Mentoring comes from two directions: the youth and the adult. When the youth starts it, the adult needs to be aware and encourage it. When the adult starts it, he can be a watchful guardian of the youth.

Many times I have seen a young person wanting a mentor. He spends time in a store, or at someone's home. He is pulled there, like a gravitational pull, not really knowing why. He just feels comfortable with this adult and wants to talk with him. The youth wants to learn to do those hobbies which the adult is doing.

The youth doesn't want to be with just anyone, so a would-be mentor can't just get rid of him and try to push him on someone else. The relationship is just the two of you, and no other. The adult who is part of this relationship should recognize this.

Adults should seek to be mentors when they can. There are many great mentoring programs (see Appendix). However, you do not have to be in a special mentoring program; often you just keep your eyes open for it. If you see a youth who could use some guidance, and if you are in the right place to do something about it, then that is the time to become a mentor.

You don't have to be perfect to be a mentor. Being a mentor is not about specific activities, it's not about money, and it's not about doing it perfectly. Being a mentor is about being there. It's about spending time.

Spend time working on the same activities, such as fishing, playing music, or fixing cars. Be together talking about nothing in particular, or saying nothing at all. Be there for birthdays and special events. Encourage him to enter a contest or play a sport, and be there when he wins the prize.

When you spend this kind of time, you build a relationship. It is during some moments of being together that the youth will ask you the tough questions in his mind, and it is then that you can offer the wisdom from your experiences. Being a mentor is not about being perfect. Mentoring is about being there for the young people in your neighborhood.

I personally believe God has a hand in this pulling of people together. You can call it what you wish; nevertheless the fact remains that mentoring a youth is a special relationship and should always be encouraged.

<u>Dinners and parties</u>

Dinners are one of the simplest ways of keeping your neighborhood together.

When was the last time you invited a few neighbors over for dinner? You do not have to make a grand formal dinner. In fact, it is better if you don't do formal dinners. Be yourself, with your own home-style cooking. Dress comfortably and talk freely. Just have good times with good neighbors.

You don't have to do all the cooking yourself. Get everyone to share in the cooking, or even make it a pot luck dinner. This makes it simpler for each person. This also gets everyone involved, which makes people feel they are a greater part of the gathering.

There are many ways to do parties. I knew one lady famous for her neighborhood parties. Each year, she would have a different theme. Decorations, costumes, and activities were for that year's theme. She cajoled her neighbors to come and take part each year, and they'd always have a good time.

Neighborhood parties are simple, fun, and effective in building a community. People bond together most easily when they have fun together. Because these parties are close to home then this makes it easier for all to attend. These aren't formal parties either, just with friends—so no dressing up and pretending to be something perfect, just come as you are and have a good time.

Parties are one of those elements which some critics will say "too simple." Well, yes it is simple—that is the point. Many communities are isolated and neighbors don't know each other. It is the simple acts in everyday life which bring a community together. Neighborhood parties are one of those simple acts.

Holidays in the community

When neighbors celebrate a holiday together, the total impact can be quite emotional.

I know of one neighborhood where each home puts an American flag in their front yard each Independence Day. Each flag is identical and placed the same way—house after house, block after block. Looking at the collection of these flags is quite stirring. They've celebrated July 4th in this way as long as I can remember, and it moves me every time.

There are also several communities around the country that celebrate Christmas together. As a neighborhood, they decorate the streets and homes. This is not just a single man decorating his house, but several blocks of homes working together to create a cohesive, decorative story. People will drive for miles to see it. They'll park their cars and walk the streets. It is a unifying event for the community that built it. Yet this is also a binding event for the larger community which comes to visit.

A community which celebrates holidays together can be quite a bonding experience.

Join groups and volunteer for the community

The community as a whole will be that much brighter if more people are involved in their communities. Churches are a great place to start. Rotary Clubs and Chambers of Commerce are also good places to know people. These organizations have multiple roles, but building a healthy community spirit is one of the primary ones.

Volunteering on projects is also good. Join a litter clean-up day. Help repair trails and fix up local parks. Dedicate a few months to coaching a sport after school, or just help with after-school programs.

Be Constructive, create solutions

Good Americans are constructive. Good Americans create solutions. They work within their communities to really make a difference. It is easy to complain, but a real American creates and implements actual solutions.

Anyone can complain, anyone can destroy, but complaining and destroying do not solve anything. Anyone can demand laws which restrict people, but how does that help the situation? Thus, an important part of the American Way is being constructive, laboring yourself, and coming up with creative solutions. This is hard work, but it is only through work that our communities become great places to live.

Each of us must work in the communities. We must get involved with helping people, and we must give of our time. We must discuss solutions with our neighbors, and we must create clever solutions to each of our problems.

It is also important that good deeds are publicized more. Every day, millions of Americans mentor our youth, help the blind, and reduce crime. Every year, Americans volunteer to clean up litter and to help in emergencies. These are the Americans who make the communities work. A few bad Americans get national attention for fighting against the American Way, meanwhile millions and millions of good Americans are quietly making a positive difference in their communities. We must give more attention to these good deeds, for each story of a good American provides hope and inspiration to others. Each good deed we learn of reassures us that America still works as it should.

There are too many bad Americans these days. They complain and fight all the wrong issues. They want to tear down our freedoms, they want to impose control over our personal lives, and they want to silence all opposition. Ah, if they only worked so hard on actual solutions as they do on destroying our way of life, then imagine what may be accomplished.

Summary of civics in the communities

An American must be civic minded in his community. Be courteous, honest, and fair. Be a friend and a mentor. Join a local church and local civic groups.

Communities do not exist by themselves. A community means people, and therefore people must take the time to nurture their communities. No matter how busy you are, no matter what your schedule is, each American must be actively involved in his community.

Civics: duties in self-government

The U.S. Constitution is just a piece of paper unless Americans act according to the words. Therefore, every American must be involved in the duties of self-government.

<u>Vote</u>

One of the greatest privileges in the United States is to freely choose our representatives. We also vote in private, so you never have to tell anyone how you voted, and so that no one can intimidate you.

This privilege is an enormous freedom. Any country which holds free elections had to go through a violent struggle to get that freedom. Do not take it lightly.

Furthermore, remember that our representatives work for us. You pay their salaries. Thus, you get equal say in hiring and firing of these people.

However, voting is a responsibility. Americans must do certain work on their own in order to vote.

You must register to vote early. All states require voters to register by a specific date, usually a significant length of time before the actual election. You must register before that date. If you do not, you will not be able to vote. There are good reasons for this. Deadlines for registering to vote are set far in advance of the voting day in order to make sure that only those who are allowed to vote are able to vote. Those not allowed to vote may include felons, illegal immigrants, and people registered in two locations. Remember, this is a law, and a wise one, so you will not be able to get around it.

Your voting card will tell you your precinct number. Note that precinct boundaries change, so check listings on the county election website for your exact voting location. Bring your card with you, for that card will allow you to vote.

Trained election personnel will check to make sure whether you are eligible to vote. They also make sure that no one votes twice.

You do not have to register with a party to vote. However, if you do register with a party, then you can vote in that party's primaries in the spring.

You must be an informed voter, studying the views of the candidates and the details of the propositions. You are allowed to take notes and printed material into the booth to help you decide, and to remind you what your choices were.

You must learn how to vote correctly. The layout of ballots and the mechanics of the voting devices are always changing. This is not new, for ballots and methods of voting have evolved throughout the history of the United States. Ballots and counting machines will continue to evolve.

Nevertheless, whatever the ballot looks like currently, you must learn how to use it. Whatever the new method of voting machine, you must know how to use it. There are no excuses for not understanding the mechanics of voting, for a team of trained election workers are always there to help you. There is no excuse for submitting a wrong ballot, and doing so will nullify your personal vote. Note that a wrong vote on your part will *not* discount the election results.

Pick up a sticker which says "I voted" on your way out, and wear it with pride. You have just completed the greatest American privilege and a most patriotic duty.

Stay informed

Americans need to stay informed about the activities of the government. Remember, the government works for us. Therefore we must always be informed as to what our representatives are doing. If we approve, then we write letters of support and reelect them. If we disapprove, then we write letters telling them our displeasure and elect a new representative.

Americans must always get accurate information. It is important that Americans use several news sources, and not just one.

In general, it is always better to have multiple sources. Good researchers in all fields know this. One source may be mistaken—that source may have only part of the information or they may be biased. This happens not just in news or political discussions, but in other areas such as heated scientific debate. Thus, for an American to stay informed on any issue, he must use a variety of very diverse sources in order to confirm that the information is accurate.

Be a responsible juror

A jury of twelve impartial peers is another great right in America. In some other countries, a person can be taken away without a trial. Men are taken to jail even if they are innocent. Therefore, a trial by jury is one of our greatest freedoms. Every man who is called for jury duty should go.

Note that being called for jury does not mean that you will serve. There are several stages of selecting jurors, some are random and some are by specific questions, and so you may not actually serve even if called.

If you do serve on a jury, you must take your duties seriously. There will be a time when the roles are reversed, and you will wish that the jurors of your case consider your case very carefully. Therefore, you should give the same consideration when you are a juror yourself.

Do not think about the work you missed. Do not think about other obligations. At this time, you have one job and one job only: to hear all the evidence, discuss it carefully, and make a verdict. That is your only job right now.

You must not only think about the particular case, but also must think about the ramifications of your decision. Verdicts in one case set precedents for the future. When you consider the case, be careful of unleashing a legal monster. Also, be careful when awarding money for damages. If the award is large, or if the person didn't deserve it, then you are just supporting theft. The ramifications of this will be examined in the section on rule of law.

Help elect representatives

Americans must help elect the representatives that they want in office. This does not just mean money, it means your time.

Let us get this clear up front: money does not elect representatives, the people do. Nobody wins elections based on money. Candidates only win if a) lots of people hear about the candidate, b) lots of people know his views, and c) the majority of people agree with those candidate's views.

This may be an oversimplification. However, the principle is truth: money is not as important in elections as enthusiastic supporters who talk up the candidate.

The candidate *will* need some money—for signs, bumper stickers, traveling expenses, and staff.

However, candidates can use other inexpensive means to get elected. These inexpensive means include: official websites; debates; bumper stickers; non-partisan reports of questions and answers on specific issues; and especially supporters talking about the candidate.

A candidate gets his message across most effectively today through his own website. Here he can place all his views and all his decisions on a thousand issues. Citizens who want the candidate to win can talk up their candidate to friends and neighbors. These citizens do a lot of talking and a lot of walking. They go to shopping malls and to fairs. They can also e-mail their friends with a little note. In all cases, the supporters can tell their fellow citizens "to learn more, read his website."

Who needs millions of dollars? What we really need most are a good website, a few signs, and lots of enthusiastic people to talk about the candidate.

Keep in touch with representatives

Americans must keep in touch with all their representatives. Remember that we hired them, and that they work for us. As any good manager in any business will tell us, we must have constant communication with those we hire.

We must keep informed of our representative's intentions and actions. We must keep informed on potential bills and on any changes in procedure that they will vote on.

We should write our representative telling him how he should vote on an important issue. We should write our representative telling him of problems that our community needs addressed. Most important, when we disapprove of an action our representative has done, we must let him know.

We should also be proud of our representatives and let them know when we *approve* of their good actions. This is often overlooked because people only think of writing when they don't like an action. Few people bother to write when they approve.

Each of our representatives gets mixed messages from his district, and if one group sends more letters, he tends to listen, even if they are physically in the minority. How is he to know who is in the majority—he can tell only by letters and phone calls. Therefore writing supportive letters and e-mails is just as important as writing when we oppose something.

Run for office

American government is run by the people. It is up to citizens to hold these offices. From city offices to state offices to national offices, it is ordinary men and women who run the government.

Any American can run for office. You can too. Ideally, politics should be a part-time profession of everyone. Each person should take an active part in running our government, just for a few years, and then go back to his regular life.

Americans often overlook the local offices. In many ways, the local offices are the most important, for they directly involve you and your community. People know of city council, but there are other elected jobs. You can run for other positions such as the water board, the school board, sheriff, judges, and many more. You'd be surprised who is on these boards and councils—often they aren't that much different from you.

Of course, not all people are interested in holding the office, even if actively involved in their communities. Nor are all people equally talented enough for the position. Nevertheless, if you have the inclination, and if you have ideas on how to make improvements in your community, then ask the people for the job. Tell the people what you will do for them, and they just might elect you for the position.

Summary of Civics

Americans must take an active part in our tradition of self-government. Be an informed voter and a responsible juror. Help elect our representatives, stay informed about issues. Communicate with our representatives constantly. Take an active part in self-government by running for office yourself.

Americans must be civically minded to ensure the quality of life in all our communities.

Patriotism

Patriotism is love for one's country and being proud of it. In America, patriotism is the belief in the American principles, and the willingness to defend them. Patriotism is a good thing, a wonderful thing, and is a significant part of the American Way.

<u>Patriotism and the American Way</u>

Patriotism in its essence means that you believe and support the American Way.

What is the American Way? Everything we discuss in this book.

Note that if someone does not support one element of the American Way, then it is usually also the case that he does not support *any* of the American Way. You can check this out for each person, for each case, and you will see this is often true.

To be patriotic, you must, by definition, support the American Way. If a person does not believe in many elements of the American Way, if he seems to be never for America but always against it, then he cannot be patriotic.
In fact, such a person is not only un-patriotic, he is a traitor. He is our enemy.

If, however, you are one of those that fully believe and support the American Way, then you are patriotic. Be proud of our country, and be proud of our American Way.

<u>The American Flag</u>

The American Flag is a symbol of America. Symbols are a shorthand way of expressing our beliefs. The American flag is our symbol representing all that we believe.

The American Flag stands for everything American. It stands for the entire American Way. When we fly the flag, we are saying that we are Americans, that we love America, and that we believe in the American Way.

There are those who destroy the flag. This makes no sense. It is due to the American Way—symbolized in that flag—that these individuals have freedom of speech and can criticize the government. It is due to the principles symbolized in that flag that they can do unpatriotic things such as burn the flag, particularly without being shot.

Anyone who destroys the flag is not merely criticizing a singular issue of contemporary America, he is really saying that he doesn't like America at all. This is not freedom of speech, this is just being anti-American, and we have to wonder why this person lives here if he hates us so.

Be proud of the flag. Fly the flag everywhere. Show the flag respect. The flag and the way we treat it symbolizes our belief in the American Way.

<u>Pledge of Allegiance</u>

Like the flag itself, the Pledge to the flag shows our patriotism. America is a wonderful country. The principles of America are so egalitarian, so peaceful, so open and rich with opportunities—there is nothing like it even today.

When we say the Pledge of Allegiance every day, we are reminding ourselves of the American principles and of the American Way. We are thankful again for what we have, and mindful of how precious it is. We rededicate ourselves each and every day to living and preserving the American Way.

The Pledge is not selective, it is inclusive. The Pledge does not just apply to one group or one person, but rather to everyone, to all Americans. All Americans should say the Pledge because it applies to them. The freedoms, the principles, and the preservation of those ideals apply equally to all Americans.

To *not* say the Pledge is to say that you do not believe in the American Way. Those people who refuse to say the Pledge or want it removed are telling us, very clearly, that they do not consider themselves American, and that they do not believe in the American Way. We must be very concerned—for if they do not believe in the American Way, then they are our enemies, and they wish our destruction.

Be proud to say the Pledge of Allegiance. Speak it loudly. Each time you say the Pledge you are reminding yourself of the wonderful American principles, and you are rededicating yourself to living out the American Way.

Fighting for the American Way

In its truest sense, a Patriot is an American who not only believes in the American Way, but also works vigorously to protect it.

The American Way needs protecting. We need patriots to fight for America—in courts, on the streets, and in battle. Other chapters will discuss this in more detail.

Summary

Patriotism is a wonderful thing.

Patriotism is love and pride for our country. We should be proud, for there is no other country like ours in the world.

Patriotism means believing in the American Way. Believe in it, support it, and be proud of it.

Say the Pledge everyday, and fly that flag high. Rededicate yourself to the American Way, each and every day.

Un-American activities and dirty words

Un-American activities

America allows many beliefs, but there are limits. You can be critical on many specific issues in America, but you cannot be critical of the American ideals.

Throughout this book I have tried to explain that there *is* an American Way. There are many aspects to the American Way, and many lifestyles and choices fit into the American Way, but there are limits.

There are certain activities and beliefs which are not the American Way. These are un-American activities, and those people who do these acts, even though they are technically citizens of America, are America's enemies. Make no mistake, their goals are our destruction and slavery.

Here are but a few un-American acts:

To burn the flag is un-American. To deny the people the right to say the Pledge is un-American. To remove God from public places, public speeches, and documents is un-American. To put down Christians is un-American. To prevent people from celebrating Christmas is un-American.

To slander, to say terrible lies about another person is un-American. To rewrite history is un-American. To steal, even through taxes, lawsuits, or welfare programs, is un-American. To support the criminal over the victim is un-American. To engage in violence to achieve goals or as a form of expression is un-American.

To over-turn a law voted for by the people is un-American. To deny the people something they want to do, through laws, coercion, or force, is un-American.

To give away military secrets is un-American. To not screen people who work in government agencies for security risks is un-American. To not support America or our troops when we have been attacked is un-American. To be silent when a member of your group behaves badly is un-American. To support our enemies, through dollars or speech, is un-American.

These are but a few of the items that are un-American. The American Way is very broad. However, there are limits to what is tolerable in America.

ACLJ vs. ACLU

The ACLU is an un-American organization. They always fight for the criminal over the victim. They fight to take away all American symbols. They fight against the people. Millions upon millions Americans oppose the ACLU, and yet the ACLU claims to fight for the people.

The ACLU is un-American because they hate America. They want to destroy us. Pay no attention to their rhetoric. They want above all else to turn America into the worst place in the world.

The ACLU is un-American because they run counter to the American people. Remember that we said the people govern themselves, that the people run their own lives and run their own communities. Hence, whatever a community wants, they should have. Whether it is customs, holidays, religious views, or laws, if the majority of the community wants something, then they have the right to have it.

In contrast to American principles, the ACLU runs counter to the people. The ACLU wants to take away the Pledge, though most Americans want it. The ACLU wants to take away Christmas decorations, though most Americans want them. The ACLU wants to take away all references to God, even though most Americans believe in God, and most Americans want those references to exist.

The ACLU is evil and un-American. They constantly fight against the will of the people. What is America about if not about the will of the people?

One of America's heroes these days is the ACLJ. The ACLJ is America's answer to the ACLU. When the ACLU picks on the American people, the ACLJ stands up to them. The ACLU manages to get money from rich anti-Americans, but there are far, far more true Americans then there are of them. It is important that citizens donate money to organizations like the ACLJ. Their website can be found in the appendix.

The People and the American way vs. PFAW

Note that another un-American organization is People for the American Way, or PFAW. Their name sounds nice, but they are anything but the American Way. Do not be deceived by their title.

If you see that a person is from this organization, note right away that they want to destroy America. Whatever they say to do, you know that America should do the exact opposite.

Good words vs. Dirty Words

Many un-American people have tried to take away good words. They have given negative connotations to many good words.

Here are some of the "bad words" as defined by the liberal-socialists, which are actually good words. You should know that these words are positive, they are good, and they make our country work better.

Shake off that negative feeling. Don't let the un-American people put that spell on you. Stand tall, stand proud, and speak these words with confidence. When all of us speak and live these words, we will break the spell the socialists have on this country.

1. Limited Government	2. Self-reliance	3. Law abiding
4. Religion	5. God	6. Faith
7. Family	8. Character	9. Ethics
10. Honesty	11. Trust	12. Integrity
13. Courtesy	14. Respect	15. Manners
16. Guns	17. Gun owner	18. Second Amendment
19. Discipline	20. Corporal Punishment	
21. Military	22. Defense	23. National Security
24. Profiling	25. Competition	
26. Conservative	27. White male	28. Cowboy
29. Patriotism	30. American	

Summary

The American Way is broad. Our nation allows more lifestyles and beliefs than another nation. However there are limits.

You cannot criticize or change the American Way. To do so is un-American. Those who attack the American Way are traitors. They are our enemies. We cannot work with them, we can only eliminate them.

We, the people, must stand up, speak out, and fight to preserve the American Way.

PART VI
Preserving and Protecting
the American Way

Rule of Law and Judicial System

Laws are an important part of every society. The people must be able to protect themselves from the criminal element. Furthermore, even the best individuals will sometimes have conflicts.

In America, we have three main elements to the system of laws: 1) the people create the laws, 2) every person is treated equally under the law, and 3) everyone has the chance to prove his innocence—usually through a jury of his peers.

All these elements are critical to a fair and democratic judicial system. The system of laws and justice is part of the American Way.

System of Laws in America

Laws are created by the people

In America, the laws are created by the people. This differs from dictatorships where laws are created by the few ruling leaders.

The people of each community decide what laws to have for themselves. In some cases, the people create laws directly by putting their own propositions on a ballot. This is democracy in its purest form. Also remember that when the people create a law in this way, no court is allowed to stop that law.

However, in most cases it is more practical to hire representatives to act on our behalf. Recall our discussion of how the people control the government—we hire representatives who act on our behalf because we cannot realistically be there. When legislators pass laws, this is still in effect the people passing laws because we choose those legislators who represent us.

Remember, that we must communicate with our legislators so that they know how we wish them to vote on various bills and issues. Legislators, too, have an obligation to communicate with the people who they represent. Always remember that the representatives work for us, and if we do not like the way they represent us, then we can replace them in the next election.

Also remember that the *legislators* are the only ones in the three branches of government who can officially pass a law. Judges have no authority to change laws or to not follow laws.

Fewer laws are better

It is always better to have fewer laws than to have many laws. The main reasons for this have to do with freedom and local control. Here are many specific reasons why fewer laws are better.

America is about freedom. Each individual ought to be able to decide how to live his life as much as possible. Therefore fewer laws are better because this allows more personal freedom.

America is also about local control first. If we have fewer laws in larger areas such as Federal and State, then the local areas can make their own decisions. When local areas have more range in governing their own communities, they will ultimately make better decisions for that community.

It is usually better to persuade on ethical issues than to legislate. Humans tend to get touchy when legislated on ethical issues. It is better to leave the ethical issue open in areas of law, yet at the same time citizens should encourage others to be ethical.

More laws mean more items that must be enforced. Those who enforce laws are busy enough. Having fewer laws to keep track of means less items the enforcers have to check on. They can then spend more time on the more important problems.

More laws also lead to a feeling of harassment by the people. The people don't like being bothered for something inconsequential. If most people feel that the law is not necessary, then they will feel harassed. Further, this tends to make the people lose respect for the authority in all issues. Yet, if we keep laws to a minimum—just the most important ones—then the people will be more likely to follow all the laws. There will also be a much better relationship with the people and the authorities.

Fewer laws make it easier for people to obey the law, whereas more laws are more cumbersome to follow. The more laws that exist mean that individuals and businesses are more restricted. Trying to meet so many laws at the same time leaves little room for progress, or even for daily living. That is why fewer laws make it easier for all laws to be followed.

With fewer laws, people can remember them more easily. Furthermore, often times a person does something for years, absolutely legal, then one day gets called on it—for it is now illegal. When did this happen? Who knows? With fewer laws, everyone can know the laws better, and thus it is easier for everyone to obey the laws.

Keep in mind that those people who make the laws and those who enforce the laws should be doing the will of the community as a whole. If most of the community objects to a law, then this means that the law is not what the people want, and therefore was a mistake.

Some laws are indeed necessary. We need laws for murder, theft, assault, slander, driving recklessly, and so on. Yet, as much as possible, we must try not to solve every issue with yet another law. Find other ways to solve the issue. We must try to persuade, to educate, and to make it easy for people to do the right thing, rather than passing yet another law.

If you serve on any law making body, always aim for the fewest laws. Do not create laws just to seem busy, or to solve every conceivable problem. Find another way.

The law is not a suggestion—it must be followed

We must clearly state: the law is not a suggestion. The law must be followed.

Liberals, socialists, and activist judges are too fond of sidestepping the law. The law is the law. You can't ignore it, or go around it. You must follow the law.

The law may indeed be a bad law. If so, then it is up to the people to discuss changing it. However, until the new law is passed, the current law must be followed.

Changing laws

Laws *do* need to be changed. Circumstances change, and times change. There will always be old issues that are no longer relevant, and new concerns arise. Thus, laws will always be modified.

In America, we change laws through the legislatures. This includes city council, the state legislature, and the federal legislature. We ask our representatives to change a particular law. The people can also put laws on the ballot for a direct vote by the people.

Laws are *not* changed by the courts. Laws are *not* changed by the press. Laws are *not* changed just by public demand. Laws are *not* changed by ignoring them.

Other groups may bring attention to the problem. However, only the legislature or a direct vote by the people can change the laws.

Equal under the law

Everyone is equal under the law. This holds on all levels: legal rights, criminal offenses, and punishments.

Everyone has equal rights under the law. It does not matter if you are man or woman, rich or poor, famous or unknown—everyone is allowed the same rights and the same privileges stated by the law.

Criminal offenses are also equal. Even if you are rich or are in a position of power, you are not allowed to break the law. You will not get special treatment for any reason. No one is above the law—not the wealthiest American, not the President, nobody.

Punishments are also equal. If the sentence is 5 years minimum in jail, then that is what you'll get. It doesn't matter how rich you are, or what your position is, you will not get special treatment or a lesser punishment no matter who you are.

It is true that some people in positions of wealth and power have escaped justice. However, this is not the American Way. It is not codified into law, and it is not part of our heritage. Those few people with wealth and power who get away with crimes are only aberrations. Most of time in this country, all men are treated equal in the legal system.

Profiling is good

This brings up the issue of profiling. Profiling is a good thing. It is a sensible thing. Liberal-Socialists will try to say otherwise, but we must not listen to them.

Profiling is well within the American Way because we have <u>reasons</u> to take a close look. We don't stop just anyone, but stop only those who fit the profile of a criminal we are looking for. Also, we stop those people who seem to fit the pattern of a criminal, catching a criminal before he actually strikes, and thus preventing the crime from happening at all.

Even when a security officer stops a man to look closer, it is just that, looking. This man is NOT just taken to jail. He is asked questions, his documents are examined, and the officers run computer checks on him. But he is not taken to jail. If this man happened to fit the profile, but is innocent, then he will be sent on his way. If, however, after the questions and checks, the police have reasonable belief in his guilt, then he is taken further through the arresting process.

Even then, when a man is arrested, there is still a trial where a man can prove his innocence. So you see, just because a man is looked at closely because he fits a description or fits a pattern does not mean he will be taken away for life. That type of activity happens in totalitarian governments, but not in America.

Note that law enforcement personnel will only investigate people who seem to be criminals. Those who work in the areas of police, security, and intelligence agencies have years of experience looking at a person or looking at information and seeing a pattern of criminal behavior. They know what type of person seems to be a criminal. The law enforcement personnel know this from years of practical experience, and in these matters they are usually right.

Most people realize the obvious: we need good descriptions of criminals in order to catch them and put them in jail. These descriptions are as objective as any scientific description, and the law enforcers use those objective descriptions to capture the criminals.

If the suspect is a black man in his 30s, then it makes no sense to look at a white man in his 50s. If the suspects are young Islamic males from the Middle East, then it makes no sense to look at Caucasian women. These actions would make as much sense as trying to catch a fish in the desert. We would never get anywhere with preventing criminals and catching criminals if we look in the wrong place.

Thus, profiling is good. It is common sense. Consider the alternative to profiling—letting criminals escape and terrorists go free. Those people who don't want profiling can only want it for two reasons: they support the criminals, or, they are criminals themselves.

Judicial systems in America

Blind Justice: equal treatment for all in the legal system

In America we say that justice is blind. This means that we look only at the facts as they pertain to the case. We are not prejudiced by whether a man is rich or poor, famous or unknown. We do not care about his ethnicity, religion, or other personal views, if they are not relevant to the case*. In America, we treat every individual equally under the law. Judges and juries are to show no partiality.

*Note that sometimes the person's views and religion *are* important, as with Islamic terrorists and communists, so we can't just ignore these all the time. There are times where religion or beliefs are central to the case.

Also in the concept of blind justice is that no man is above the law. It does not matter what position of power you have. It does not matter how much wealth you have. The law will treat you equally. A man who is rich or famous must face the same punishment for the same crime as a man who is not well known or is not rich.

This may seem odd, particularly after seeing the cases such as the offenses of Bill Clinton. However, these are aberrations. These are specific cases where justice in America failed. That is why many Americans are angry. A few men escaped justice, and escaping justice is not the American way. Therefore, every time Americans see a lack of justice, Americans should double their efforts to ensure that justice will prevail the next time.

Unfortunately, judges are not always fair themselves. This is not the American Way either. There are many judges, such as several in California, who have bias for one person over another. These judges have been known to not hear evidence from one side. They have been known to rule in favor of their preferred side even with flimsy evidence. Judges such as these must be removed from office and never be allowed to be a judge anywhere again.

Nevertheless, in spite of these aberrations of the system, the ideal of the American Way still exists: equal treatment for all people in the judicial system.

<u>Chance to defend yourself, with appeals; assumed innocent</u>

In the American system of laws, a man is presumed innocent until proven guilty. This is important. It is up to the prosecutor to prove guilt more than it is up to the defender to prove innocence.

Also, in America, you have the right to defend yourself. This is a precious right, one still too uncommon in the world. In other countries, if you are accused, then you are hauled off to jail. Sometimes you are never heard from again, left in jail to be tortured and die.

In America, you have the right to defend yourself. If you can't afford an attorney, you are entitled at least to a public defender. Even if you lose your case, America has a system of appeals so you can have more chances to prove your innocence. This is a great privilege, one that is wonderfully democratic. Contrast this to being hauled off in the night and never being heard from again—as often happens in other countries—and you will rarely complain about being mistreated in the American judicial system again.

Trial by Jury

In America, we have a great system of trial by a jury of our peers. If you get a trial by jury, then you are assured that the people will hear your case. The people, not a king nor an appointed judge will decide. This is a far more democratic method, for it is a system of justice administered directly by the people.

Jury duty is an important responsibility. If you are called to jury duty, you should always go. If you are intelligent, well-read, hard-working, and honest, you will be a great asset on the jury.

Often, juries make bad judgments. This is because juries are generally not educated. We must rectify this by educating more of our citizens, by giving the people a better general practical knowledge of more subjects. Thus, the more a person knows about a topic before being a juror, the better juror he will be.

However, do note that in many cases, a judge alone is all you are allowed to have. His or her decision in the matter is final. Personally, I am not altogether pleased with this situation having seen the bias by many judges over the years. The people must have a more effective system for removing biased judges.

Maxims regarding laws and the criminal element

Maxim #1. There will always be a criminal element. However, there are always more good Americans then there are criminals.

Corollary #1. To stop criminals, we must merely band together and stand up to them. We must also do this continuously.

Maxim #2: There is no tool which cannot also be used as a weapon.

Corollary #2: We must not outlaw a tool outright. If we did, then we'd lose the benefits of the tool.

Maxim #3: For any area where there is trust, cooperation, fairness, or justice, this area will also be a prime area for the criminal element to invade.

Corollary #3: We must be aware of the criminal element, yet we must also hold on to trust. We should devise approaches which allow trust, fairness, and cooperation to flourish, yet punish an individual case of criminal behavior before trust erodes.

Maxim #4: For any illegal activity, someone will find a way to profit from it.

Corollary #4: Making an activity illegal is not necessarily the best strategy.

Maxim #5. No matter how sophisticated the set of rules are, the criminal element will find a new way to use the rules for criminal purposes.

Corollary #5: We should not over-legislate. We do not want to encumber the many good citizens merely due to a few persistent criminals.

Summary

In America, laws are created by the people. Many times the people initiate and vote on a law directly. More often, due to reasons of practicality, the people hire representatives to make laws on behalf of the people in each of the legislatures.

Fewer laws are better. Americans must keep as much personal freedom as possible, and local control always provides the best solutions. Fewer laws enable these to be a reality.

There will always be a criminal element, but there are always far fewer of them than of decent Americans. We should be careful to not over-legislate and not encumber the many good Americans with a quagmire of laws just for the sake of catching a few persistent law-breakers.

In America, everyone is treated equally under the law, without consideration of anything that is not relevant to the case. Status, money, or power will not protect any American from justice.

If accused, you are presumed innocent until proven guilty. You have a chance to defend yourself, usually judged by a jury of peers. A system of appeals and the guarantee of a public defender ensure that everyone has opportunity to prove his innocence.

Being a juror is an important responsibility. Americans must go when called, and must take their duty seriously.

Laws can only be written by the people or by the legislature. Courts cannot change laws. Laws will always need to be modified as times change. However, there is a correct procedure for doing this—and the courts have nothing to say in the matter.

The government is not above the people

In America, the government is run by the people. As such, no government worker or representative is superior to the people.

In America, nobody is above the law. Laws apply equally to everyone, no matter what position or how much money a person has. In terms of the government, nobody, including the President, can break the law.

The government works for us

Our representatives work for us. They are agents, who represent us because it would be difficult for us to be there in person. As such, they are employees—they work for us.

Being our employees, they are not above us in the law. In fact, because they work for us, we are above them! Few people remember this.

No one is so important that he cannot be replaced

Anyone can be replaced. Americans in all professions are quite aware of this—even CEOs and movie stars get replaced.

The same holds true for the government. No elected official—not Governor, not Senator, not President—is beyond being replaced. They must run for re-election, and can be replaced then. They can be impeached. They can be recalled by the people.

If any representative is breaking the law, if he is behaving in a grossly unethical manner, or if he considers himself more important than the people, then he can be thrown out by the people and be replaced. There are always many qualified

Americans for each of those jobs. No man is so special that he cannot be replaced by a better representative.

Trying to get away with it

Many government workers and representatives try to break the law and get away with it. Many in government in the past twenty years, usually Democrats, have thought that they were above the people rather than working for the people. They have behaved in astoundingly unethical ways, and have broken many laws. In many cases, they have harmed their country. Here are a few real examples to clarify the issue.

Bill Clinton

Bill Clinton is a classic example of a man who thought himself above the people, and he was the worst President in our history. We must never elect another one like him.

Let us look at just the one act where we have solid evidence of his guilt: sex with an intern in the Oval Office. Just about sex? Hardly. It is about one man thinking he is above the people.

1. The White House is not the President's private house. This house belongs to the people. The people let him stay there for free, and the people pay for all the servants and maintenance. It is not a private house.

2. The White House is also a place of work, especially the Oval Office. Furthermore, this is a place of doing work for the people. This is not his private area in any way.

3. Having sex at work is sufficient reason to be fired. In any job in America, if you had sex at work you would be fired immediately. The President should be no different.

4. Having sex with an intern is sufficient reason to be fired. Any non-professional relationship between intern and superior can put pressure on the professional relationship. In any job in America, just flirting with an intern could get

you in trouble, and one date or one sexual relationship is certain to get you fired. The President should not be treated any differently.

5. Lying under oath is perjury. For our court system to be effective, everyone must tell the truth. Lying under oath is a serious offense, and any American who does this is sent to jail. The President is no different. He lied under oath, and therefore he should have gone to jail for this act.

So you see, in this one case Bill Clinton committed many offenses. Employees in businesses would have been fired, and any American who perjured himself would have been sent to jail. He was hired by us to do work for us; he is not above us.

There are other offenses of which there is no doubt that Clinton did. One offense was that Clinton did not let the FBI screen people for security risks who worked in the White House.

This should be an obvious thing to do, and for many years past the FBI had been screening employees who wanted to work in the White House. The White House is a central point to our government with many security secrets—the potential for compromising our national security is enormous.

After the terrorism acts of September 11, 2001, we wonder how much our nation was put at risk by Clinton not allowing these security investigations to go through. We must also wonder why he let so many people work in the White House without having to go through these security checks. This President may have put our nation at great risk.

Clinton did other offenses, some of which are not provable but point to him. Many books exist on the subject. The evidence may be circumstantial, but coupled with known un-American acts many of these other offenses are likely to be true.

Bill Clinton thought himself above the people, but in our country, no one, not even the President, is above the people. This is why he was impeached. His friends in the Senate prevented him from losing office, but many ordinary Americans think that he should have been fired and thrown in jail. No one is above the law, not even the President.

Texas Democrats

The Democratic representatives in Texas left the state twice over a redistricting vote in 2003. They thought they were better than the people.

The background is simple. The U.S. Constitution stipulates that a Census be taken every ten years, after which new district boundaries are drawn according to changes in populations. Every state must do this every ten years, and it usually works well.

According to Texas State law, a vote cannot be taken on certain items, such as redistricting, unless there are a certain number of representatives. The Democrats didn't like the proposed redistricting boundaries. Hence, the Democrats left the state of Texas, and thus according to law, no vote could be taken.

The Democrats did this to try to force changes of the district boundaries more to their liking. The flaws in their logic are many, including that the Republicans who are now the majority managed to be elected using the boundaries drawn by Democrats ten years earlier. Also, many of the redistricting areas have had a significant increase in population—hence the new boundaries reflect that—just as is supposed to happen.

More important than the issue of redistricting is the issue of Democrats leaving the state—and hence leaving their job. Any American would be fired immediately for not showing up for his work. Yet these Democrats still keep their jobs. Not only do they still keep their jobs, but they get paid while not showing up for work, and they run up costs in overtime (billed to the people, of course).

The Texas Democrats think they are above the people. This is evident by them not showing up for work and still getting paid. This is not the American Way.

Legislators robbing the people through taxes

If you want more money, you can't just take it from another person. That is robbery, and you will go to jail. Yet, when the government wants more money, they just take it from the people by forcing them to pay more in taxes. This is still robbery, and our legislators must not be allowed to get away with this. Legislators who demand more taxes think they are above the people. They are not.

Summary

The government is *not* above the people. The government is run *by* the people. Those who work for the government in fact *work for* the people. No one in government is allowed to act in any way contrasting with the ways of the people—legally or ethically. Anyone who does so can be replaced.

Punishing bad behavior and illegal acts

In order to preserve a civilized society, we must punish immoral behavior and illegal actions. This is part of the American Way.

Actions must have consequences. If there are no consequences, then the world is just a free-for-all where anyone does as he pleases. Without punishments, criminals will continue to hurt and steal from others. Without punishments, criminals have no reason to stop. This is not the American Way.

We have seen too much of this in our nation today. Too many unethical acts and illegal deeds are not being punished. Too many bad people are getting away with hurting good Americans, and thereby also destroying our country. This has to stop. We will make it stop.

There are three basic levels to punishment: deterrence; rehabilitation; and removal from society.

Level 1: Deterrence

We want to prevent people from doing criminal and unethical acts. Ideally, we would like no bad behavior at all. This is deterrence.

The first way to deter is through teaching. Teaching ethics is so important that many people must be involved. Parents, churches, civic groups, schools, and writers have the greatest influence in teaching ethics.

We teach morals, and we teach right from wrong. We teach about laws in our community. We explain why good behaviors benefit all of us, and why bad behaviors are wrong.

Most Americans are basically good, and most people will understand ethics when explained to them. Teaching of morals is enough for most Americans to do the right acts most of the time.

However, in order to fully deter, you must also have consequences. These consequences are extra incentives for people to not behave in the wrong way. In addition, many people will have to face these consequences a few times before they are fully deterred for the future.

Here is one example of how deterrence can occur. A parent teaches his children that it is wrong to steal, and he explains why. He further states that if he catches them stealing, they will have to return the item to the person stolen from, apologize to that person, and then be grounded for a week. The children nod their head and understand. They do not steal. This is effective deterrence through teaching ethics and stating consequences.

However, further suppose that in a few years one child is caught stealing. The father again explains why stealing is wrong. He then follows with the punishment. As stated earlier, the child is taken to the person he stole from, returns the item, and apologizes in front of all. Also as stated earlier, this child will be grounded for a week.

Due to following through on these punishments, the child is less likely to steal in the future. (There is no guarantee he won't—but he is less likely to do so.)

Punishment effective for that person

In order for punishments to be effective, they must be relevant to that type of person.

A young child cannot reason, so spanking is effective. A teenager can reason, but if reasoning is not enough, a more effective punishment is to curtail his social life and remove privileges. Businessmen are deterred by threats of being sued. Physical labor can be effective punishment for many ages and many crimes. For more hardened criminals, jail time is often the only effective punishment.

Punishment fits the crime—a teaching method

Whenever possible, the punishment should fit the crime. The main purpose behind this is to teach a lesson. When the criminal's punishment is related to the crime he committed, he learns more clearly why his behavior is wrong, and he is less likely to do it again.

For example, a person who litters is required to pick up trash for several days. Studies have shown that those who pick up trash are less likely to litter because these people have done the labor to pick up the trash left by others.

This may not be possible for all crimes, but punishments which teach should be sought whenever possible.

Parental rights to discipline

Parents have the right to discipline their children in any way the parents want. Government has no place telling a parent how to discipline his child. No member of the community has any right to tell a parent how to discipline his child.

A good parent disciplines his child. We must always remember this. These children are well-mannered and ethical. They are better students and more successful as adults. They grow up to be model citizens in every way.

In contrast, children without consequences at home grow up to believe that no consequences apply to them at all. They grow up to be selfish, aggressive people, and they disrupt the community throughout their lives.

As a teacher I have seen both sides many times. Where there are consequences at home, these youth are well behaved and more studious. Where there are no consequences, then these youth are disruptive, aggressive, and fail their classes.

The need to discipline children was considered common sense for many thousands of years. It is only over the past forty years that misguided people have tried to declare discipline to be a bad word. Forty years has been plenty of time to see the folly of no discipline. Without punishment at home, people become selfish and aggressive. With punishment at home, people become polite and ethical.

The critics of discipline have these wild imaginations of excessive beatings. However, these are no more real than the imaginary monster under a child's bed. Good parents know how to discipline their children. These parents are firm and they are creative. They do use physical methods when necessary. The children learn their lesson, and are less likely to misbehave again.

Thus, in the great majority of homes in America where parents discipline their children, these parents discipline effectively without being excessive. The excessive beatings occur far less often in real life than in the wild imaginations of the critics.

Furthermore, America has decayed over the past forty years, and significant reasons include not enough discipline and fewer punishments. Thus it should be plainly obvious that we must have more discipline and punishments in order to get America on track again.

Government and the community must stay out of the area of parents disciplining their own children, allowing these parents do what they feel is best. When society removes the stigma of discipline, then parents can think freely about how to punish their particular child for a particular offense. Parents who feel more free to discipline their children are more likely to do so, and will be more effective.

Americans used to know a common expression: spare the rod and spoil the child. We must return to this common sense perspective in order to raise good Americans for the future.

School discipline

School discipline is very important. As a teacher in public schools for many years, I know full well the seriousness of this issue.

In the schools of today, the students have all the power while the teachers have none. The solution to school violence and aggressive youth is simple: 1) give teachers more authority to discipline students, and 2) offer more real discipline options. That is the exact solution—yet it is the only solution that schools don't want to hear.

Students today are aggressive—much more aggressive and violent than in our past. What can a teacher do? Basically…nothing. If a teacher even touches a student, then that is considered an offense. Never mind that the kid threatened other students. Even if the student gets disciplinary action, not much happens. Consequences such as detention or being talked to by the principal mean little to the aggressive student.

Thus, there are few real, meaningful consequences for the aggressive actions of these students. Without meaningful consequences, we will not be able to deter bad behavior and violence in the schools.

So, how to combat aggressiveness, disruption, and violence in schools? Let's start by supporting the teachers when they discipline. Then, let's expand the options for disciplining students.

As for specific disciplinary techniques—we need more discussion. Discussion today is limited because the schools silence speech on the subject. If you even mention the topic, it could mean losing your job. Yet, in private, the teachers themselves are talking of practical solutions.

There are many good ways to have effective school discipline. What are those ways? I know of a few, as proposed by teachers in private discussions, but we still need more open discussion on the issue in order to get the best ideas.

Level 2: long term punishment and rehabilitation

The second level of punishment is long term punishment. The great majority of crimes fall into this category.

The goals at this level are several:

1) Punish the criminal in such a way and for a long enough period that he really hates his punishment.

2) Convince the criminal to do better. There needs to be a point where the criminal says to himself "I never want to go through this again."

3) Rehabilitate criminals to start a new life. We always hope that a criminal will grow weary of his punishment and not want to go through this punishment again. We help this criminal adopt new habits, live a new lifestyle, and learn new skills.

The punishments must be severe enough that the criminal really despises the situation. Only then will the criminal want to be good. It doesn't matter if he isn't altruistic yet. If avoiding jail or physical labor is an incentive to not repeat the crime, then that is incentive enough.

The length of punishment must be a balance. The time must be long enough for the criminal to really hate it and want to change his ways. Yet also, the time should be short enough that the criminal can start a new life should he really want to.

Level 3: removal from society

Some crimes are so heinous that punishment must be severe and long term. Some criminals are such hardened career criminals that there is no chance of reforming them. Some individuals are so cruel and evil that they cannot be allowed in society. For these reasons, we must have long term punishments for the most serious offenses.

Crimes that fit into this category include multiple premeditated murders, treason, and repeated aggravated assault. Punishments for these crimes can include a lengthy sentence in prison, or the death penalty.

Summary

In order to preserve a civilized society, we must punish immoral behavior and illegal actions. This is part of the American Way.

Actions must have consequences. There are three levels of punishments: deterrence, rehabilitation, and removal from society.

People who are punished are more ethical and well mannered. Discipline leads to better citizens. This is the American Way.

Preserving the American Way at Home

Because America is based on self-government, then preserving and protecting the American Way is done primarily by individuals and the community.

The spheres of influence, working outward

The American Way is preserved and protected by these groups, in the following order: individual; family; community; civic organizations; city government; state government; federal government.

Individual

The American Way starts with each individual. The following statements are the personal ideals that I hold myself to. I hope that these will be your standards as well.

As an American, I must try my best at all times. I must try to be honest, hardworking, fair, and courteous. I must be respectful and polite. I must try to be friendly and helpful to all. I will join others, for social or civic reasons. I will try to be a welcomed member of all my clubs and communities.

I must work to create my own success. I must make my own choices, and I must accept ownership for all of my decisions—whatever the results. I will try to pursue my happiness in my own way, yet try not to hurt others in the process. I will try to take life's struggles in stride and try to have a sense of humor about it all. I will try to keep my faith, as is my beliefs, to carry me through the most difficult times.

I will call attention to actions that harm others or are destructive to America. I will do my best to live by the American Way, preserve it for the future, and protect it from our enemies.

Family

Families are an important social unit. Families are more than relations by birth, they must also be a foundation for life.

Whatever happens in the home will affect the community. That is why it is essential for parents to teach values. Children must learn to be responsible and respectful. They must be well-mannered, courteous, and honest. Parents must live these values as an example, and discipline their children as needed.

All family members must share the regular chores. Note that sharing in chores is the basis for all of America. In the family, sharing chores means each member doing his part to help make his family better. In America, sharing chores means each American doing his part to make his community better. This habit of sharing the chores for the good of all is a habit that is best developed early.

Families must spend time together. The more time a family spends together, the stronger they will be. It is vitally important that a family is strong. The first line of defense against the problems of life is the family. A person needs that place to come to. Every American needs a place where he can get advice, love, and assistance. A strong family is such a place.

A family is like a safety net. One relationship is like a rope, connecting two people. That is a good thing, but one is not enough. However, build many of these relationships and you have a safety net. You will have a crisscross of interlinked relationships, just like a crisscross of interlinked ropes. Now you have a safety net when you really need it. Whenever you have a serious problem, your fall is far less painful, and you can recover more easily.

Perhaps most difficult for a family is this: all family members must try to both deal with realities of life and at the same time nurture the family bonds. Real people and real life situations make the ideal family a constant struggle. Yet it is a struggle which is worth the effort.

Also remember that the relationships that you have with each family member will go through cycles of being close and being strained. Never give up completely on a member of your family, and be open to the possibility of getting close again.

Families must aim for the following: open communication, compromise, listening, understanding (even if disagreeing), supporting each other, working through issues, and, most difficult, forgiving each other. These goals are not easy, even for the best families. However, the benefits of a strong family are so important that all Americans must continually try to keep their family relationships strong.

With the disintegration of the family, and with more people thinking about themselves first, where does one go when problems arise? They go to drugs, violence, therapy, welfare, and entitlements.

Lack of strong family has led us to a fragmented society where social problems have increased dramatically. The government has increased in size to tackle these problems.

This is not the way it was meant to be. If we get back to a traditional structure of stronger families, then everything will fall into place. Individuals will be happier, there will be fewer social problems, and the government will shrink down. Everything right now has grown out of control, but with a return to the solid family unit, most of America's troubles will collapse back down to normal scope and size.

A strong family is essential to a good life, and is an essential building block of the American Way.

<u>Community</u>

Communities take care of themselves. We discussed much of this in the chapter on being a good neighbor.

Basically, Americans must have positive relationships with their neighbors. They spend time together socially, they respect each other, and they help each other. Local neighborhoods can be a wonderful place. However, we must remember that communities are people, not buildings, and therefore people must spend time with their neighbors, not shut away indoors.

Civic Organizations

To get things done for the community on a large scale, we need civic organizations.

A civic organization is essentially a group of people who want to do good for their community. The causes are endless—for every community issue, there is an organization that looks into it. Nor is it just service, for the members have fun times as well as doing good deeds.

Remember that in America the people take care of themselves. Remember that in America we believe in limited government. Yes, Americans care. Yes, we are generous. But no, we do not believe the government should be involved in charity or welfare. It is up to the people to take care of their own communities.

These civic organizations do many things. Many organizations raise money for diseases. Some organizations work to raise the youth with good morals. Other organizations work to reduce crime. Some organizations reduce drug abuse, while other organizations increase literacy. The great things that these civic organizations do are amazing.

Yet, we must emphasize, that the organization is still just the contact point. It is the people themselves, the people of the community, who make these things happen. The people are the ones who selflessly donate their money. The people are the ones who give so much of their time. Without these people, the organization would be just a name. It is the people of the communities who make the results.

Thus, civic organizations are the idealized form of self-government. They are larger than family or local neighborhood, so they can coordinate larger projects and coordinate larger distributions of money. Yet they are not the government. These organizations provide services for the community, but they are not paid for by taxes. No one of the community is forced to do anything, and yet good Americans willingly do so many things. That is why I say that all these civic organizations, together, form the idealized form of self-government in America. Civic organizations are people voluntarily taking care of their own communities.

<u>Governments—city, state, federal</u>

After the primary levels of individual, the family, the community, and the civic organizations, then, and only then, does the government get involved.

The people see where the government is better able to do something for the community than individuals. However, there should always be local control first and foremost. We have talked about this elsewhere.

Preserving our Communities is up to Us

Preserving the American Way is up to us. It is up to us, the ordinary people, to keep our communities healthy.

To anyone who is disturbed by something, I ask: what did you do to try to change it? If you are seriously bothered by something, and you feel that it is not being changed, then you should work to change it yourself. If you are not proactive, then you have no right to complain. In addition, when a group of people with the same grievance join to become active, you should join them. When they offer suggestions for improvement, you should listen and support them.

The community and country in which we live is ours. It belongs to me and you, and we want it to be as beautiful as it can be. To do that, it is not enough for individuals to act alone. Everyone must be involved.

It is not merely the responsibilities of legislators, clergy or a few leaders to work for our community—each of us must work for our community as well. If each of us looks for improving the quality of our community when we interact with it, then the overall quality of our communities will be improved. Each person should select an issue to work with, and join a team of others with the same vision so that progress is always made.

You may think that your influence is small, but in fact anything you do for the community will be more effective than you think. There are many reasons for this:

1) One man cannot be everywhere; therefore we need as many people as possible to be a guardian of values. We need many people to be mentors, many people to watch for criminals, and many people to help their neighbors. Together, we can take care of our communities and take care of each other.

2) Slow progress is better than no progress. Remember that whatever you have to give, whenever you can give it, will make improvements. If each man calls attention to a problem, and does his best to fix it when he can, then progress will continually be made. Furthermore, if everyone is involved, then one person will take the up the task where another has left off.

3) One small step, one small change, is worth a great deal. All any of us can ask for is one small change, one step at a time.

4) There will always be people who are afraid to do something other than the norm and who are afraid to take risks. We must persuade them to care, and we must lead them to take risks which will benefit everyone. If one person makes one small change, then that one person provides hope and courage to others.

Thus, preserving the community and preserving the American Way is primarily up to the people. We must take care of our communities, and must do it ourselves. You may think your one act is small, but that is really how America works. America's communities remain healthy by individuals taking care of their own communities, in small ways every day.

Community Leaders

Although the people must be involved, there indeed must be a few people who step up as community leaders.

Community leadership

One misconception about community leadership is that you must be totally devoted or not do it at all. This is not true. In the best world, many people in the community take turns leading the various organizations.

Devote a year or two in a leadership position, then hang back and be just a member of the group. After a few years, go again for a leadership position.

Whether it is the Chamber of Commerce, Rotary Club, City Council, or a mentoring program, take an active role for a year, then take a break. On your break years, be involved with your personal life and your family. Continue to be involved with your community organizations, though on a less frequent basis. After a few years, step up and take the leadership role again for another year.

When the jobs of community leaders are shared by many people of the community, then it is easier for everyone. In this way, no one citizen is over-burdened, and community spirit remains vibrant.

Church leaders

Church leaders also have important roles. The clergy work to keep the people focused on God. They remind people of the morals to live by, and the difference between right and wrong. Other church leaders, the laymen who are not ordained but take leadership roles in the local church, also play important roles. They serve important functions through getting people involved in the community.

Activists

There are some people who are so devoted to their community that they devote most of their time to it. These are community activists.

"Activists" have changed in meaning over the years, so we must be clear on what we mean. There are good activists, and there are bad activists. Good activists fight for the American Way. Bad activists fight to tear the American Way apart.

In my other book, Making America Great, I talk in detail how people who care about the American Way can do things to actively change America. Note that you can work your regular job full time and yet also be effective in fighting for the American Way. Again, that book, Making America Great, has all the details.

Here I will emphasize things that activists must *not* do:

1. No violence or vandalism.
2. No hateful speech.
3. Do not fight against any principles of the American Way.
4. Do not fight for anything counter to what the people want.
5. Do not be disruptive—outside, inside, anywhere.
6. Do not take away anything the people want. Add your desires to it.

Most good Americans believe in the American Way. Yet they are busy working, being involved in civic groups, and spending time with church and family. Only a few good Americans are activists for the American Way. Contrast that with the most full time activists. Too many full time activists are actually people who want to destroy the American Way. As the webmaster for the eminutemen, I am all too aware of their destruction. They work fast and steady. Some of us good activists fight the bad activists full time and we still can't keep up.

That is why it is essential that all good Americans become serious about the internal threat to this country. At this point in our nation's history, all good Americans must become active to protect the American Way. The enemy is here in this country, not just out there in other countries, and they have been very successful. I believe that we *can* stop them. I am certain about that. Many of us work hard every day to do just that. Yet, we cannot work alone. Until this threat is gone, all good Americans must join the fight, in a very active way, otherwise there will be no America left to fight for.

Police and the Government

In order to preserve the American Way, we sometimes need more than the community—we need the force of the government.

Remember, the government is the people. However, the police are both representatives of the people and a greater force than the people. We give them certain authorities over all of us, so that we can live our lives without fear.

As the scale of crimes or un-American activities grows, so must the level of the group who takes care of it for us. City police, state agencies, FBI, Department of Homeland Security…we need all of them.

Remember there will always be criminals. There will always be people who want our wealth and people who want to destroy the American Way. Whether this criminal is a local threat or a national threat, whether he uses weapons or uses the courts, we must fight to preserve the American Way and must fight to keep the peace. Where the people as individuals or as community groups are not effective in stopping the criminal element, then the people give authority to others to do the job. The group involved depends on the type of activity and on the scale of the act.

Thus, we the people hire others, and give them authority in certain areas, so that all of us can pursue our happiness in peace. We do this so that our communities are safe, and so that our American Way is not damaged.

Summary

We must preserve and protect the American Way. This starts with you, the individual. You must live your life and interact with others in a manner that is fitting of your privilege as an American.

The family is the most basic social unit in America. In families, values are preserved, work-ethic is learned, and relationships are built. A strong family makes a strong safety net. With strong families, more people will be happier, most social problems will decrease, and the government can reduce to normal, limited size.

Communities are where America really happens. Everyone must be involved with their neighbors, and with their community as a whole. In order for a community to be a good one, everyone must take an active part. This includes knowing your neighbors, helping others in need, and doing regular tasks such as reducing crime and improving education.

Civic groups and churches are contact points for people to take care of their communities. Everyone should take a leadership role, even if it is just for a year or two.

We need more people who are activists. However, they must be activists for America, not against it. Further, American activists must still behave in an ethical manner while attaining the goals.

Where the people as individuals or as community groups are not effective in stopping criminals, then we give authority to specific government groups to take care of it. We need them to prevent and stop the criminal element.

America is only as good as its people. We the people must preserve and protect the American Way here at home.

Protecting America Abroad: Freedom Isn't Free

Introduction

Freedom isn't free. In order to preserve our freedoms, we must protect them. Enemies from around the world want to destroy America and our freedoms. It is only through the U.S. military that Americans can feel safe and secure.

No one wants to go to war. However, there are times when it is necessary. We should always first talk with these nations, discuss the issues, and try negotiations. Yet many times these negotiations fail. They fail primarily because the other side is not interested in peace; they are only interested in our destruction. Therefore, we cannot live with these people. We must destroy them in order to protect ourselves.

The United States never conquers. Unlike many other nations in history, America will never be an empire. We seek only to protect our own nation, and to preserve our way of life. We even assist other nations, helping them become as free and as prosperous as America. However, if any nation or rogue group plans on hurting us, we will destroy it. It is a case of self-defense, and this is part of the American Way.

Wars are necessary to protect our nation. Without our well trained military, without our patriotic men and women protecting us, we would not be able to enjoy the bounties of this nation.

Fighting Early

Americans must fight early. We must not wait. Intelligence gathered by our agents keeps us informed. When we know of threats, we must stop them. We must not let them grow.

Furthermore, we must fight to win. We must fight using overwhelming force, and we must encourage people of the local area to fight on our side. To repeat, we must fight to win.

<u>Why other countries hate us and why we go to war</u>

There are many reasons why people around the world want to destroy us or conquer us. It is because of these reasons, we must fight. Note all these reasons are a version of self-defense.

1) Jealousy

Many people are jealous of the United States. They are jealous of our success. These people are vandals. They think: if I can't have those great things, then I don't want America to have them either.

They falsely believe that the reason they are not successful is because of the United States. These people don't realize that we had to create our own success. They don't realize that self-government is not easy. They are not aware that creating a successful business is hard work. If these other countries want what we have, then they must work like we did. Even if they destroyed us, their problems would still exist. Therefore, anyone who harms Americans because of jealousy must be stopped.

2) Misinformation

Many countries see only part of what America is about. Many people of the world get their views of us from the movies and television we send abroad. Is it any wonder they think Americans are crazy and immoral? Even many Americans here don't like what they see on TV and movies these days, but the people of the world don't know that.

Further adding misinformation is the lack of free press. Dictatorships around the world control the radio, newspapers, and television. The people see only that of America which the dictators want the people to see. The people are told that the United States is evil, and the people of these dictatorships have no proof otherwise. Because these misinformed people see us as evil, they are easily led into fighting to destroy us. We must stop them.

This is why free speech is so important in every society. Champions of free speech have countered the controlled press in these dictatorships through creative means. In recent years, free speech and information have come to the people of dictatorships through satellites and through the internet. Exchange student programs also help greatly to dispel myths about America.

3) Power
Dictators want power. They control their own people, they control the government, and they conquer more people and more lands. Dictators are never satisfied—they always want more control and more power.

All civilized nations should come to the aid of those nations being conquered. This is best done by nations in the regional area, but America can assist in many of these endeavors.

We must defend ourselves, for eventually the dictators will come to us. Hitler would have loved to come over and conquer America, as would Stalin and the Emperor of Japan. Therefore Americans must go to war to protect our own borders from being invaded.

Remember those who sacrificed. Freedom is not free.

We must always remember those who sacrificed for our freedoms.

Many people gave the ultimate sacrifice—their lives—so that America could be free. Many more have returned home less whole—losing legs, hands, and their sight—so that Americans could be free.

Even those who return physically whole are sometimes suffering mentally. They function well, no doubt of that, for most American soldiers are proud and stoic, and do not complain. Yet these Americans saw blood and death—sometimes caused by their own hands. It is not easy for many of these patriots to forget those images.

I am always amazed when I talk with a veteran. They are the most patriotic and stoic individuals I know. I am amazed to know of the suffering that a soldier has gone through because of his wounds, and yet he still lives a full, self-reliant life. I am amazed to hear some of the things that a soldier has seen regarding war, and yet he keeps those experiences to himself until asked about directly, and even then will talk about it only in private conversations.

Veterans often have the best understanding of the American Way. Talk with an older veteran, one who has lived a full life, and you will find more insight regarding America, and a greater example of the American character, than you could ever imagine.

We must remember all those Americans who have fought for the American Way. We must think about all those patriots who fight to protect us today. These patriots leave home, at a young age, to fight in strange lands thousands of miles away. They have a job to do. Yet they are disciplined and ready to do it. They face the enemy in order to protect the rest of us. They are prepared to kill the enemy as they need. These men and women are prepared to come home permanently damaged by battle. These Americans are ready to die for our country.

Would you be able to do these things? As for myself, I do not think I could do what our soldiers do. I will be forever grateful for what they have given us. I will be forever grateful for the freedoms we have, and for each soldier's personal sacrifice.

It is in part because I know that they have given so much, and because I know that what I do cannot compare, that I try to keep the American Way alive. We will continue the fight to preserve America—at home as well as abroad.

Summary

Much of the world does not understand America. We must try to explain the American Way to other nations. It is also best to encourage them to adopt our principles so that those countries can be as free and as prosperous as we are.

However, there are times when we must go to war to defend ourselves. There will always be people who want to destroy us, usually because of jealousy or misinformation through propaganda. In addition, there will always be people who want to take our wealth and conquer us.

Nevertheless, we should never compromise our way of life. Nor should we hesitate to defend ourselves. We must also do this early, when problems are still on a small scale, in order to prevent larger threats to our security.

For all these reasons, Americans must go to war to defend our freedom.

Ethics in America

Introduction

Ethics are very important. We live a life of quality only if we live ethically. We are designed to be happier and more satisfied when we behave ethically. Communities and nations function better when everyone acts ethically. Businesses thrive and economic prosperity exists for more people when we act ethically.

The Constitution gives us freedoms. However, it is our ethical culture that has really made our nation great. If we were not ethical, we would not have the comforts or the prosperity. If we cease to be ethical, then we would soon lose the prosperity.

America is perhaps the most ethical nation in the world. I have traveled, and I have seen many things. I have yet to see any nation that has such strong ethics as America. I have also seen that America has the most reliable infrastructure and the most prosperous people. It is a combination of freedoms and ethics which has continually made our nation a more perfect place than anywhere in the world.

Immigrants come to America, and that is fine. However, many immigrants do not adopt the ethics and manners that we have here. There are two problems with this. First, if we dilute the ethics of the people who live here, then we dilute the ethics of the entire society. This degrades the overall quality of everything within America.

Second, think for a moment—why do immigrants come here instead of staying in their own country? We must have something that works. Does it make sense to destroy what works? Of course not.

Therefore, we must insist that American culture has distinct ethical principles. We must insist that all Americans live by these ethical principles. This is necessary for America to always be as great as it has been.

One final point on ethics. There are two sets of ethics—a universal set, and a set that is debatable.

Debatable ethics: There are some ethics which are debatable—such as alcohol being a sin, or the boundary between privacy and public security. Yet, do not confuse those ethical dilemmas with the absolutes.

Universal ethics: There *are* standards. There *are* ethical ways of living that you *must* practice if you are an American. Many cultures over many centuries have derived similar principles. These are best for us—as individuals and as a society—and have proven to work. We cannot have moral relativism. There are some absolutes. These absolutes are the American Ethics.

Lists of Ethics

Many cultures and groups have come up with lists of ethical principles. I have found that many of these lists are similar. Here are just a few of my favorite lists.

A. The American Character

Honesty, Trust, Fairness, Courtesy, Respect, Tolerance, Kindness, Generosity, Equality, Integrity, Self-reliance, Obeying of Laws, Active in the Community, Laughter, Optimism, Faith.

B. Boy Scout Law

A Boy Scout is: Trustworthy, Loyal, Helpful, Friendly, Courteous, Kind, Obedient, Cheerful, Thrifty, Brave, Clean, and Reverent.

C. Leander School District, Ethical Principles

Honesty, Integrity, Promise-Keeping, Loyalty, Concern for Others, Law abidance, Civic Duty, Respect for Others, Fairness, Pursuit of Excellence, Accountability.

D. <u>Cardinal Virtues</u>

Note: since these terms are old, a brief clarification follows each.

Prudence—common sense, judgment, intelligence
Temperance—moderation
Justice—not only courts but also fairness, honesty, keeping promises
Fortitude—courage, persistence

Note: Cardinal is *not* a religious term. A better translation today would be "pivotal" or "primary."

E. <u>The Ten Commandments—focusing on the last 6</u>

5. Honor your father and your mother.
6. You shall not commit murder.
7. You shall not commit adultery.
8. You shall not steal.
9. You shall not give false testimony against your neighbor.
10. You shall not covet anything that belongs to your neighbor.

Note that I focus on the last 6 because these are universal. The first 4 talk of God. I want to emphasize that there are universal morals on those ancient tablets, even without the top 4 which refer to God.

F. <u>Ben Franklin's List of Virtues</u>

Temperance, Silence, Order, Resolution, Frugality, Industry, Sincerity, Justice, Moderation, Cleanliness, Tranquility, Chastity, Humility.

G. <u>Gene Autry's Cowboy Code</u>

1. A cowboy never takes unfair advantage.
2. A cowboy never betrays a trust. He never goes back on his word.
3. A cowboy always tells the truth.
4. A cowboy is kind and gentle to small children, old folks, and animals.
5. A cowboy is free from racial and religious intolerances.
6. A cowboy is always helpful when someone is in trouble.
7. A cowboy is a good worker.
8. A cowboy respects women, his parents, and his nation's laws.
9. A cowboy is clean about his person in thought, word, and deed.
10. A cowboy is a patriot.

<u>Summary</u>

Ethics is very important. Ethics is central to the good life for all individuals and for all of American society.

We must teach ethics. We must teach ethics by posting ethical principles followed by teaching specific examples.

There are many good lists of absolute ethical principles. I have given a few lists in this chapter for your use. It is now up to you to live up to them, and up to you to teach them. Post these principles in highly visible areas. Teach these ethical principles to everyone you can, using many specific examples.

Teaching the American Way: Courses in Civics and History

Introduction

In order to preserve the American Way we must teach it. We must teach courses in civics and in history. We must teach these to a variety of people, at a variety of levels. This is the only way to ensure that America will be just as great in the future as it has been in the past.

Do not let America become like the pyramids of Egypt

We must teach the American Way to all new generations of Americans and to all immigrants. If we do not do this, then our great civilization will be lost.

Let us take a warning from the ancient Egyptians. What do I mean? Look at the great pyramids at Giza. No one knows for sure how they were built. Scholars have various theories, but no one knows for certain. If we fail to teach about America, eventually no one will know for certain how America was built either.

The pyramids are great wonders, standing for thousands of years. They shouldn't be there, and yet there they are. It seems impossible for such heavy stones to be moved. It seems impossible for the structures to have such geometric precision. Even by today's standards they are a wonder. It is impossible, and yet, there they stand before us.

We don't know how the Egyptians built those pyramids. Furthermore, it is unlikely that anyone today could build them with just the same materials and technology. No one knows how.

Yet, at one time, someone knew how—probably thousands of people knew how. If the ancient Egyptians had taught their children, and their children's children, then surely we would know today. But they didn't teach their children, and so we don't know. Their great creation stands as a puzzle.

We must be wary of this, and not let America become a mystery. Great men and great women created America over a period of many years. How could any nation be so free, so egalitarian, so peaceful, and so prosperous? It shouldn't be here, but here we are. Like the pyramids, this seems impossible. Yet, like the pyramids, America stands before us.

We must teach new generations how this country was formed so that it is not a mystery. We must teach about the American Way so that future generations can create just as much prosperity and happiness as anyone in our history. We don't want America's greatness to become a puzzle.

If we teach civics and history, then the American Way will endure, and the people will remain prosperous and satisfied. However, if we do not teach these things then our great America will become like the pyramids—an inanimate puzzle. Like the building of the pyramids, scholars would have their theories about how America became great, but no one would know for sure, and thus few would know how to make America great again. We must not let that happen.

We must teach civics and history to all new generations and to all immigrants. This is essential for the survival of America, and for the continuing endurance of the American Way.

Types of people to teach

Because so many people need to be taught the American Way, and because this often requires different courses for different audiences, we should look at the various types of people who need their own civics and/or history course.

Students—jr. high

Teaching the American Way must start early. We must have some preliminary civics along with the American History at this age.

Students—high school

We must have a semester long course just on civics at a high school level. This was standard years ago, but today most schools have dropped it. We *must* require all high schools to teach civics, and that means a course devoted solely to civics.

It is essential to have a course devoted to civics because civics is a complex subject. The American Way evolved over many years, with much discussion and debate. The Colonials lived it and discussed it for over a hundred years before the revolution. Even during the founding days, some of the most brilliant minds of the time debated issues for days at a time. The American Way cannot be fully understood by new generations in just a day or two. It takes time to really understand the American Way. As such, it is important that a full semester be devoted exclusively to teaching the American Way.

In addition, high school students should have two semesters of American History. In this, students should learn of all history that is relevant to the creation of the American Way.

Students—college

All colleges should require a civics course. At this level, civics instruction can be more sophisticated, discussing more complex issues. A good course should also encourage involvement in the community in some way.

Colleges should also require advanced courses in American history. There is so much history to learn of this country. Therefore, the more history that students learn, the better all of us will be.

Immigrants—exchange students—high school

Exchange students come here to learn about America. Therefore, they should learn civics. If all high schools require civics, as it should be, then the exchange student can take this class during his year in America.

Immigrants—exchange students—college

Many college students in America come from other nations. These students come here for a variety of reasons. Some stay for only a year, while others stay the full time and earn a degree. Some of those who earn a degree here go back to their country, while others choose to stay in America.

It is very important that we teach civics to these students. There are many reasons for why this is important. First, we like to have these students because they can learn about America. When they go home to their country, they have a better understanding of America. This understanding of America is usually quite a bit more than what their people normally learn about. In this way, even more people have a better understanding of America.

Second, our ways of democracy, free enterprise, and egalitarianism are great ideals. If more people around the world learn about the American Way, then they may be more likely to adopt it themselves.

Finally, if the students choose to stay here, then they want to become Americans in the fullest sense. However, before they can be part of our culture, they must understand our ways thoroughly.

For these reasons, it is very important that we teach civics to exchange students.

All universities which have students from other countries must require that they take courses in civics. There should be two courses. One course should be the basic level of civics, the level already taught to Americans in jr. high and high school. The second course would be the same college level civics course required for all students.

Immigrants—to keep visa, as long as they are here

Immigrants who work here, whether they plan to stay here or not, must be required to take civics courses. In order for citizens to keep their work visas, they must take civics classes for many years. There are many essential reasons for this.

This issue is so important, that we expand on this below.

Immigrant Workers and Teaching the American Way

<u>Reasons to mandate immigrants take American Way courses</u>

1. When an immigrant wants to works here, he must get along with other Americans. He must speak English well enough to communicate. He must understand our customs and manners. This is not unusual—an immigrant worker to any country would do the same for that country. Therefore, we must teach them the American Way.

2. Many immigrants today steal from America. Many are just here to take advantage and to have their way. They do not come here for the opportunity to create success, but rather for the systems which permit taking from others. This is *not* the American Way.

3. Many immigrants today believe in a class system, and are opposed to democratic ideals. These views take our society backwards hundreds of years.

4. Many immigrants today believe Americans to be stupid because they are fair. Many immigrants think Americans are weak because they are polite. These views are bad for America. These immigrants must be taught the American Way so that they know that these views are not acceptable.

5. What if the worker wants to become a citizen? If he is to become an American, he must fully understand the American Way. In America, the people run the government, and the people run their own lives. Therefore it is imperative that this worker be taught, in detail, all aspects of the American Way before becoming a citizen.

6. We must also teach the immigrants in order to teach the families of the immigrants. The immigrants who stay here a long time often have families—either their own children born here or relatives brought in from their native country. If the immigrant has no understanding of America, then his family won't either. We have just perpetuated the misunderstanding, and have further taken the greatness of America down a road of decay. If, however, we teach the immigrant properly about America, then he will teach it to his family. Then, the American Way continues to be taught and spread throughout all the people of

this country. So, it is very important that we take the time to teach civics properly to all immigrants.

7. What if the worker wants to go back to his country? The immigrant worker should go back to his home more informed about America than before he came. Many countries have limited information or spread propaganda about the United States, and therefore any immigrant who understands us correctly will be able to explain us better to the people at home.

Structure of Mandated Courses for Immigrants

I envision an on-going mandatory course for immigrants to learn civics. Both government sites and private schools could offer these courses. These immigrants must pass certain levels in order to keep their visa status. After failing three times, they can no longer stay here.

The course needs to be on-going and with many levels. This needs to be ongoing because there is much civics to know.

Consider the ideal American civics education: one semester civics in high school, one semester civics in college, two semesters American history in high school, one semester American history in college, several years of English learning to read and write, and several hours of civics and history in jr. high.

This amounts to approximately four years of one hour classes, or about 800 hours. Note that these hours and courses are for Americans who were born here and raised with the American Way as a culture. It is that much more difficult for immigrants who come from a completely different culture and have difficulty with the language!

I don't think we should ask less of immigrants than of those born here. Whether you are here by birth or by choice, whether you stay a year or a lifetime, all Americans must learn civics and history. Americans must learn approximately 800 hours worth of American history, English, and Civics. This may seem like a lot, but it really isn't. In fact, many good Americans learn even more and about civics—through active participation, and throughout their entire life.

Furthermore, the percentage taken of a man's life for these studies is small. A simple calculation: one year has over 8,000 hours, and five years has over 43,000 hours. So, what we are talking about is less that 1% of a man's life for those few years. This is a small price to pay for being an American!

This course must be on-going because immigrants stay here for different lengths of time. If you are here only one year, then you only need to take one year of civics. Yet if you wish to be here for the rest of your life, then 5 years is just a blip to you as you later become a proud American citizen.

Ideally, these courses should be paid for by the government (and yes, this means the tax payers). You have read much of this book, so you know I believe in limited scope of government, and I believe in limited government spending. However, I believe that teaching immigrants about the American Way is very important to our nation. Therefore, we must require it.

I would like immigrants to pay for it, yet many will not be able to afford it. I see this as totally different than health care or social security, for it is essential to teach immigrants about America. America's greatness will follow if we teach it to all who live here, just as our demise would come if we do not teach it. Therefore, I believe this is one of the few things important enough for Americans to pay for.

Being an American is a privilege, not a right. Anyone who lives here must believe in the American Way, or not live here at all. Requiring 3–5 years of civics courses, one night a week, is a small cost to immigrants for the privilege of living in America.

We must make this a requirement for visa status so that immigrants will go to these courses. Immigrants will know this before coming here, so there are no surprises. If they choose not to show for class a number of times, they must go back to their country. It is that simple.

Immigrants—large businesses

Immigrants who work here must learn about the American Way. We discussed all the reasons why above.

Many large businesses hire foreign workers, and if they do, they should make it a requirement for the job to take civics classes. As with connecting courses to the visa, the course will be connected to the job: immigrants will lose their job if they fail to show up for class.

Large businesses can further help America, and themselves, by offering civics courses at their site. The actual teachers can be brought in from nearby schools. Yet, having courses at the site makes it easier for immigrants to take, and takes less time out of their day.

Ideally, America should have mandated civics classes, and ideally paid by the government (we the people). However, until long term civics courses are a visa requirement, large businesses should step up to the plate and make it a job requirement.

What to teach regarding the American Way

This book itself is designed to teach people, of all ages and backgrounds, the many varied aspects of the American Way. By reading this book, Americans will have a much better understanding of the spirit of America. With this book, I want to help preserve this great nation for generations to come.

In addition, civics classes must spend time studying the Constitution and other founding documents. Students must read the famous speeches and the famous books. Civics classes must look at personal behaviors, at community issues, and at the levels of government. A good civics course should also get Americans involved in their community and their government.

American history classes must teach the founding of this country and biographies of American role models. A good history class will teach not only the major events of history, but also teach the history of the people.

There are millions of American stories, with many Americans living the American Way. I would like to see the short biographies and histories complied by family historians, and to have these become accessible to the world of education. Genealogy groups would make collections of these family stories easier to find and to buy. Libraries would have many of these collections on CD-ROM. Teachers and students would know where to find these stories.

I would also like to see these stories become a greater part of history education in America. Real Americans have given us examples of many of the principles in the American Way. Some of these examples include: winning against the odds; holding onto morals; creating success from poverty; neighbor helping neighbor; communities that pull together; fighting for our freedoms; and innovations and creations. From these American stories, we learn of our character and learn of our strengths. From these true lives we learn of heroes who were ordinary men, and we become inspired to move optimistically into the future.

As with all items regarding education, we must make certain that students are indeed taught principles regarding the American Way, and not taught socialist ideas. To ensure this, we must have people who understand the American Way in the positions of authority regarding curriculum. Also, as citizens, we must scrutinize all areas of education, and we must demand the replacement of anyone who does not uphold the American Way.

Summary

In order to preserve the American Way we must teach it. We must teach it to the youth, and we must teach it to the immigrants. We must also remind each other of the American Way, for even the best of Americans can become forgetful. This is the only way to ensure that America will be just as great in the future as it has been in the past.

We must teach new generations how this country was formed, so that it is not a mystery. We must teach about the American Way, so that future generations can create just as much prosperity and happiness as anyone in our past.

We don't want the keys to America's greatness to be hidden. We want everyone to know the way. In fact, we want other countries of the world to become as successful as America.

Whether an American was born here or came as an immigrant, whether he is here for a year or a lifetime, he must learn civics and history. All Americans must learn Civics, English, and History, approximately 800 hours worth in total, to really understand the American Way.

Books such as this one will help explain the American Way to future generations. In addition, Americans must read the major documents, books, and speeches of our heritage. All of these American concepts must be discussed, examined, and then lived.

Modern Issues and the American Way

Introduction

There are modern issues that fit into the American Way. Some of these are due to our technology and lifestyle. Others are due to the fact that we are reaching the limits of our resources. Still others are modern threats to the very existence of the American Way.

Some of these issues include: privacy, immigration, terrorism, energy, and the environment.

Detailed discussions of these issues require separate books. A few have been written, and I plan on writing detailed works on these issues myself. There are also websites which cover these issues. You can find some of these in the appendix, and more information on my own websites.

Here in this book, we will discuss some of the main points of these issues as they affect the American Way.

Privacy

Privacy really is a basic right. If the Founding Fathers could have seen the issue today, I believe they would have listed the right to privacy as a fundamental right in the Bill of Rights.

We cannot go back in time, but we can protect ourselves for the future. I firmly believe that the right to privacy is such a fundamental right, that we need to state it in law. Furthermore, our right to privacy is one that is being trampled on daily, and to such a degree that we need an Amendment to the Constitution guaranteeing a Right to Privacy.

The first hint at privacy is in the Fourth Amendment, which says that no one can enter private property without a warrant. However, issues of privacy have gone beyond that.

Much of a person's history is open to the public, though should be kept private. Furthermore, the government not only releases public records, but even sells them. This is fundamentally wrong.

In the spirit of the American Way, only those people with specific areas of authority should have the right to look into a person's history. This includes school records, rental history, property ownership, and medical records.

Business people also do sneaky things, which should be illegal. Companies track visits to websites. Companies buy and sell lists based on products you buy. These practices must be made illegal.

In the spirit of the American Way, marketing people must *not* be allowed to gather personal data, or sell information on you. Companies must try to sell their product through traditional means, such as through advertisements.

Immigration

Immigration is a problem for two main reasons: 1) we have limited resources, and 2) many recent immigrants destroy the American Way. We also now have this issue of terrorism.

A large problem is illegal immigrants. The un-American people call them "undocumented workers." Some also say "they just don't have their papers." This sounds nice, but it really means that they are criminals.

Remember that they came here illegally. The obviousness is so dumbfounding it is often hard to articulate: what part of "illegal" do you not understand?

I don't care if they want to work, you have to follow the law. As a teacher, I had to get certified before I could teach—a process of courses and tests. I would have skipped all that trouble if I could. I just wanted to work honorably as a teacher, but I couldn't without going through the process, that would be illegal.

The same could be said for doctors. Imagine this scene: a doctor without a degree. The doctor just wanted to help people, he just wanted to work. What difference does it make that he never attended medical school and never got a degree? That is called "practicing without a license." Not only is this a criminal offense, but you probably would be glad someone stops him from doctoring without a license.

The liberals would tell us, he just doesn't have his papers, right? He just wants to work, right? He just wants to help people, right? What is the big deal? Well, it is a very big deal, for every profession, and for every American. We cannot just break the law because we find that it is in our way.

Further, if we give a pass on someone who breaks the law, that makes a mockery out of our entire legal system. People from around the world see this free ride, and then come in illegally. Furthermore, people start to break other laws—and why shouldn't they, if they don't get punished.

No, "illegal" means exactly that. "Undocumented" is just a different word for "broke the law but wants a free pass."

The basic solutions to the immigration problem include these:

1. Slow the immigration rate. It would be good to stop it altogether for a while.
2. Teach the American Way to more immigrants.
3. We must be strict on illegal immigration.
4. Screen immigrants more thoroughly before we let them in, and keep better track once they are here.

Terrorism

Terrorism is a major threat today. However, keep in mind that the existence of people who want to destroy America is nothing new. It is the type of threat that changes. When the era of terrorism is over, some new form of threat will arise.

The creation of the Department of Homeland Security was a great step. That will coordinate information more effectively.

Other steps include:
1. Fighting terrorists on their lands, before they reach the U.S.
2. Stop allowing illegal immigrants to enter.
3. Screen immigrants more thoroughly, and track them while here.
4. Profile. Yes, look closely at all people from Islamic nations.

Energy

We like our energy, and there is nothing wrong with that. Energy allows air conditioning in summer and heating in winter. It allows refrigeration of food as well as the appliances to cook it. Energy lets us have cars and computers; it lets us communicate more easily, and allows us to live more comfortably. To repeat: there nothing wrong with using energy.

However, we must create energy in order to use it. Furthermore, as population increases, we must naturally increase our energy supply.

We must eliminate many of the regulations on energy creation. Only then will we be able to create enough energy to meet demand.

Energy *can be* environmentally friendly. Technology improves all the time. The creation of energy is much more environmentally friendly than it was 50 years ago. However, few people know this because this issue is not discussed enough.

Energy will be the new economy, particularly electricity. Every city needs electricity, so there will need to be a plant and wires needed for each city. Furthermore, we need more plants, many of which can be small, local plants. All of this means employment for each local community.

To repeat, we must have energy for our modern society. Energy production is far more environmentally friendly than people think, because the technology has advanced. New companies and new jobs will be created around the energy industry. This will be one of the main pieces in the new American economy in all major cities.

The environment

The environment is vital to our health—clean air, clean water, and good soil for food. The environment is also a beautiful thing, an element of the world that greatly adds to the quality of life. Therefore, we must protect it.

Americans of the past did not have to think about the environment. However, we are reaching our limits, and therefore we must be careful.

We *can* have business and the environment. We *can* have the comforts that we enjoy and still keep our forests and city parks. This is achievable. I discuss the details of this in my other book "Making America Great". I will also write other books detailing this important topic.

Technology and American know-how will get us there. The key is to make solutions practical, make them easy, and make them economical. Here are but a few examples.

Recycling has become commonplace because it has become so easy to do. With many businesses and waste disposal companies offering sorting bins, recycling is easier for the people to do, and is more cost effective for a business to collect.

From cars to ovens, our technology makes better and better use out of energy, and thus a better savings on the environment.

Even Ben Franklin, the quintessential American, used American know-how to help us in this area. His stove made heating more efficient, and thus used less wood. Franklin himself specifically noted that this device saved trees in many towns throughout the Colonies.

There are many more examples. I will detail more such examples in another book. The point is simple: we can preserve our environment and enjoy our comforts. We can have our environment and have our modern life. American technology and creativity are the keys. We merely have to be creative and be practical.

Summary

There are many modern issues facing America today. This is but a brief glance at the major points of these important issues.

Property Rights and abuses of Eminent Domain

Introduction

Property is sacred. Owning property is one of the unspoken desires of many who wish for the "American Dream." Yet according to the Constitution, the government has the right of eminent domain—which means taking private property for the public good.

This worked fine in 1789. It is far from good today. Land is far more limited today. Furthermore, there are many abuses of eminent domain. Therefore we must have changes in laws to reflect these issues.

Property is a man's dream for life

Property, such as a house and land, is much, much more than a mere possession. Homes are areas where people spend their lives. Homes are where memories are created. Homes are places which families can enjoy for generations.

There are many Americans who believe in putting down roots. To them, their land is not just any spot, but *the* spot—for life. Those who think this way spend a lot of serious time looking. They look throughout a state, and even at different states. They pick their spot of land very, very carefully. They choose their spot based on what they envision as their dream lifestyle.

In addition, a man may build his dream house. He *plans* his home. This won't be a standard floor plan which most people are forced into, no, this will be designed just for him. No other house would be the same.

Thus, taking land from us is not like taking a car or a chair, which are replaceable. The spot where a man builds his home is *the* spot—the one he searched for carefully. His home is the spot that he planned on enjoying through old age, and the spot that he wants to give to his grandkids.

Taking land or a home is much more than the taking of any other property. Taking property really is taking someone's life away from him. It is not far off from sending them to prison, or shipping them off to live somewhere else. That is something dictatorships or socialist countries do. This is not something usually done in America—but it is.

To repeat: land and homes are not mere possessions—they are part of a man's life.

<u>Americans work hard for property; expense</u>

In 1789, land was not a concern. There was so much land that it cost very little to get a piece. Many poor immigrants and many poor farmers were able to get a piece of land without too much trouble.

This is not so anymore. Land is expensive. To buy land now is like buying an airplane or a yacht. Land today is a very expensive item. Land is now a luxury that few can afford.

Thus, in order for any man to get land today he has to work hard. A man suffers a lot today for just a few acres of land. He gives his soul. Therefore, it is wrong for any government to just come up and take it.

A man's land can be taken only if the use is truly needed by the public, and, only if this spot is really the only option available. If not, then this man and his property should be left alone.

<u>Land is limited today</u>

Land is ever more scarce in America today. For hundreds of years we had plenty of land. This is no longer true. The building of freeways and large shopping centers has had much to do with that. In any case, we do not have the land that we used to have. We cannot be as cavalier about paving over nature as we once were. We cannot be as cavalier about eminent domain as we once could.

There is a need to keep up with the needs of the people. We do need homes, businesses, schools, and other buildings for the public. However, we must also realize land is limited.

The "Public Good" includes more open land

The public good does not just include roads, but also includes trees and nature. Thus, if we are considering "the public good", then we must consider that having more trees and more wild land is a large part of the public good. In fact, having more wild land is many times more in the "public good" than another freeway.

Also note that once land is paved over, it is gone forever. Concrete that is placed is rarely removed. Thus, paving roads and building large structures equal permanent death for our natural world underneath. We must remember this.

Eminent Domain basics

According to the Constitution, the government is allowed to take any private property and claim it for public use.

All of this is stated in the 5th Amendment. There are several items in the 5th Amendment, the most famous of which is not having to testify against yourself. For reference, the item on eminent domain in the 5th Amendment reads: "...nor shall private property be taken for public use, without just compensation."

The principle behind this is that there are public needs, such as courthouses, schools, and roads. This is fine, as long as the scope of taking property is limited. However, the government has been abusing its authority of eminent domain for too long, and this is why we must adjust the legal parameters of eminent domain.

Currently, any government can take land. City, county, state, and federal governments all have authority to take a man's private property. That's the bad news. The good news is that the person must be paid for his property, and paid a fair price for it. The payment of fair price is guaranteed in the 5th Amendment of the U.S. Constitution.

Again, the intention is fine, but there have been many abuses, and these abuses must be stopped.

Abuses of eminent domain

Cities have been known to take property for very bad reasons.

Many cities have taken property and given it to businesses. These cities claim that good business is good for the economy, and hence taking homes from people is in the public interest. All of us want a good local economy, but not at the expense of the residents.

Even green land not yet built on is taken too quickly. A recent disheartening example: a public park was taken and sold to a business. I used to watch local people play baseball there many times. Now it is a car dealership.

Other cities condemn a nice, old area of town. These homes are often good quality. The houses are real houses, not like the ugly houses created today. Often the owners have lived there for years, they have maintained the area, and everything is very nice. Yet these cities condemn the property, claiming it is too old or is a blight. This property is then given over to developers—to make cheap houses, or to make a shopping mall.

Then there is other property which is taken for social engineering or liberal views of the world. Property is taken away from people just to save a tiny salamander or to house yet another government program—often not wanted by the people in the first place.

Remember that the definition of eminent domain includes this concept: that the property must be used for the interest of the public. These abuses are *not* in the interest of the public. How can it be, when you are taking away the property *of* the public?

Rushing too quickly to take land, other ways to do things

The government—all levels—rushes too quickly to take property. Because of eminent domain, they have power. They can take any land or home on a whim, and are answerable to nobody. For them, it is an easy way out to many problems.

It is an easy way for those in government to get what they want at the expense of the people.

Remember, land is scarce, land is expensive, and property is sacred. To take land is akin to sentencing a person to death. You have taken a life from someone by kicking them off of their dream. You will have torn down trees and paved over the grass, never to be seen by anyone again. Yes, eminent domain equals death sentence. We must keep that perspective.

Also, consider this perspective: in the real death penalty, a person often spends 10–20 years on death row before the final event, and during this time, he is allowed to go through many appeals. This is not so with eminent domain—a person's land can be taken within a few months, and appeals are very difficult.

Therefore, when we consider taking property, we must do so very seriously. We must first look at alternatives. Taking property must always the last option, and must be considered a very grave affair.

<u>Other ways to get same needs done</u>

Here are but a few examples of alternatives to taking land.

1. <u>Instead of building or expanding yet another road, invest in high speed rail</u>.

Public transportation *will* work, if we make it work. There are many, many people who would use high speed rail rather than drive. However, you have to build a realistic, reliable system first. Only then people will use it.

2. <u>Look at previously used sites or barren sites.</u>

In every city I've been to, I have seen used and barren sites. These sites are perfect for locating the needs of the public. These include: former quarries and mines; old businesses gone bankrupt; and areas too rocky or too dry for most people to want to live there.

Bankrupt businesses are already paved—you are not hurting the environment by using them. These sites are also in town, close to the people, and so they are good locations for schools, police, firehouses, courts, and other public agencies.

Areas that are too rocky or dry are perfect for roads and schools. By taking the dry area, you are less likely to take from a citizen. Furthermore, if you choose dry and rocky areas over green areas, you will have not affected the environment as much.

Reclaiming land is also a wonderful thing to do, for we use the land more than once. Old quarries are great sites for utilities, schools, or businesses. Many of these areas can be completely reclaimed, with new vegetation, new animal life, and grassland for new homes.

In most communities, there are areas that are naturally less desirable for living. Choose these sites for roads, rather than the preferred green areas.

3. <u>Sharing sites</u>.

Government offices can share sites. Social services can share sites. Look for creative ways where the government can use buildings for multiple purposes, even sharing with businesses, rather then taking property for a new building.

4. <u>Claim land after a natural disaster</u>.

When a disaster hits, such as a flood or tornado, then a person's home is already destroyed. He won't mind moving at this point.

Consider offering a cash settlement to each resident who has been affected. In turn, the local government will get property to keep in its reserve of property. This property can be used for any of the eminent domain needs in the future.

Note that the price offered *must* be the price for the home as it was in good condition. We must pay him fair price—which is the cost to rebuild or to buy a new home. This is no time to take advantage of him economically. The only point of asking for the land after a disaster is that the man has lost his home anyway, so he may be ready to move.

This list is not exhaustive. As with many issues, we can find solutions if we are creative. We must stress that all government agencies must look carefully for creative, alternate solutions for their eminent domain sites.

Laws needed to limit abuses of eminent domain

1. Eminent Domain laws must be rewritten to specifically state what uses can and cannot be considered eminent domain. Property can be taken for eminent domain for purposes of: schools, utilities, and transportation. Property cannot be taken for purposes of private businesses or redevelopment.

2. Eminent Domain laws must state that the government must try other solutions before seeking to claim property for eminent domain. The government must prove to the landowners that all other options have been considered.

3. Eminent Domain laws must mandate that property can only be taken if the property owner agrees, or if the people of the community approve of it through a direct vote on a November ballot.

Summary—Property is sacred

Property is sacred. It is more than a possession, it is man's life. It is his hard work and his dreams, it is his memories and his legacy.

Property is expensive today, and land is very limited. Therefore we cannot be as cavalier about taking property as we were in the 1700s or 1800s.

We must view the taking of a man's property the equivalent to death. The man's hard work, his lifestyle, and his dreams are taken away. His life is interrupted. The land will be paved over, and forever lost to the people. Therefore, all members of government must view taking property through eminent domain as a grave business.

We must write laws, at all levels of government, to stop the recent abuses of eminent domain. We must also write laws stipulating that other options must be considered before resorting to taking a man's personal home.

There are plenty of alternatives—we just need to be creative and be willing to use them.

Improving America

Introduction

The principles of the American Way work very well. However, the details will need to be adjusted. Technology advances. Circumstances change. In addition, our society is continually evolving to living up to our ideals. Therefore, although the principles of the American Way are firm and perfect, the details of our lives will need adjusting.

There are ways to do this, and ways not to do this.

I have devoted an entire book to the subject of making improvements in America. This book is titled <u>Making America Great,</u> and it details how each American can improve America. The techniques described in that book are realistic, easy, non-violent, and are things which any ordinary man and woman of America can do.

Here I will highlight some basics, as it pertains to the American Way.

<u>Improving America, in the spirit of the American Way</u>—list in brief

1. Evolution, not revolution
2. Persuasion, not litigation
3. Peaceful communication, not violence
4. Work with businesses, not against them
5. Discussion with many people, not mandating by a few
6. All the community involved part-time, not just part of the community involved full time.

Improving America in the spirit of the American Way—details

1. Evolution, not revolution

In America we believe in evolution, not revolution. Only the socialists believe that revolution is necessary.

It is always best *not* to have revolutions. Revolutions disrupt society. They cause chaos. It is better to evolve gradually, slowly.

Consider an individual person on the path of change. People change slowly, requiring time to adjust to a new path. Throw a man into the end of the path cold, and the shock could destroy him. So it is with society—we cannot just impose change. If we did, people, businesses, and society in general couldn't handle the shock. Therefore, we must change society in an evolutionary way.

Socialists will tell the lie that most great changes required a revolution. This is a big lie. The truth is that most of the successful changes in America were done by *evolution*.

Pick any topic and you will see this is true. Voting rights for women? Changes came in steps, that is, through evolution. Curing diseases and expanding the length of the average life? Changes came in steps through evolution. Flight technology from the Wright Brothers to the Space Shuttle? Changes came in steps, through evolution. Quality control in most businesses? Changes came in steps, through evolution. Reducing litter and increasing how much we recycle? Changes came in steps, through evolution.

I could go on and on. America believes in evolution. America progresses in all areas by peaceful evolution. America can do this because of the great nature of the American Way. Our freedom of speech, our free market economy, our democratic form of government, and our freedom to live our lives as we choose—these elements altogether give the people the power to make changes in many areas without the need for revolutions.

It is through small steps, over a period of time, that we get from here to there. That is the American Way.

2. Persuasion, not litigation

Due to the nature of self-government—both governing oneself and running the government—people are mostly free to do as they wish. Therefore, litigation is not the answer to getting desired behavior. Litigation is not the answer to ethical issues or to bad choices that people make. Litigation in these matters is not the America Way. The better approach is to persuade people.

Sometimes laws *are* necessary. We discussed this in the section on Rule of Law. Remember that it is up to the people of each community to determine when laws are appropriate, and when laws are not needed. Also remember that fewer laws are always better, and in issues of behavior, persuasion is preferred over litigation. Persuasion is the ideal American Way.

3. Peaceful communication, not violence

Americans have different views on many issues. To resolve these issues, we can assemble peacefully and use our freedom of speech: Through freedom of speech, we learn facts. Through freedom of speech, we have vigorous debate. Through freedom of speech, we arrive at the best solutions.

However, at no time in these discussions should an American ever become belligerent or violent. If your idea is truly the best, then your idea should carry itself. Your idea and your persuasive abilities will carry your ideas through to the people.

Furthermore, a violent nature only hurts your cause. The more violent you are, the more people will turn away from you. In addition, the people know that if you do not have faith enough in your idea on its own, (evident by resorting to violence or slander rather than discussing ideas) then the people know there must be something inherently wrong with your ideas.

To repeat: the American Way is for people to communicate freely, but in a peaceful way. Americans may exchange ideas and try to persuade others. Americans must never be violent or engage in hateful speech, for such aggressive behavior will only turn people away from your cause.

4. <u>Work with businesses, not against them</u>

Businesses are a reality. This is not a bad thing—it is a way of life for all civilizations. For thousands of years, everyone has been in some form of business. People make goods and then trade their goods for money or for other goods. This is how people get all the food and all the goods that they need. Trade is also the way people make money. It is the way people survive, and then further, thrive. Therefore, destroying business does no good to anyone.

Furthermore, in America anyone can start a business. In other countries this may not be so easy, but here in America, starting your own business is pretty easy. In America, many small businesses grow to become great successes because of the free market.

Note that more Americans work for themselves or for small businesses than work for large corporations. Most of American workers are very close to the business. To many Americans, success or failure in business is very personal. Therefore, we always want businesses to prosper.

There are, however, good things that businesses should be doing. Businesses should be safe for the workers, good to their employees, good members of the community, and not too harmful on the environment. These are just a few ideals.

Yet at the same time, we must create a balance. We must make all ideals economically workable for the business. It is not enough to complain about a business, you've got to propose a solution that is workable. It is not enough to destroy a business; rather you should come up with a realistic alternative. It is not enough to demand environmental constraints; you must make sure that these are realistically achievable.

Thus, you should work with businesses when you want change, not work against them. You must create solutions yourself, and help implement these solutions. It does no good just to protest or demand laws—you must offer a real alternative. If a solution is economical, realistic, and not too difficult, then many businesses will gladly go along with the idea.

5. <u>Discussion with many people, not mandating by a few</u>

The best solutions are going to come from gathering many people. To create the best solutions to any community problem, you must: gather a set of people with diverse backgrounds and diverse skills, educate them on the facts, and then discuss thoroughly. Realistic solutions to any community issue—no matter how complex—can be created in this manner. (For more details, read <u>Making America Great</u>). This is the American Way.

There are those people in power who think they know best, without talking to anyone on the street. People in positions of power—in any industry or government—are away from the people. The people in authority do not deal with the subject matter everyday, as many of the citizens do. Therefore, their solutions often are flawed—and obviously flawed to the average citizen.

In contrast, the people of the community know the issue much better. For every issue, there are ordinary citizens who work with this issue every day. They are the ones who know what works and what won't.

To repeat: a few people with power dictating to others will never be as good for the people as a vigorous discussion with many common citizens who work with the issue first hand. The American Way is to discuss the issue with many people before proposing any solutions.

6. <u>All the community involved part-time, not just part of the community involved full time.</u>

It is not enough for a few leaders to be involved. Every American must be involved.

Some examples: If everyone keeps his area clean, then the whole community will be clean. If everyone watches for crime and reports it, then there will be fewer criminals on the streets. If many people mentor the youth, then more youth will be good citizens.

The American Way is for each American to be involved in his community on a part-time basis throughout his life. Whatever the issue, the concepts are the same: the more people involved means that the work is shared, and will not be a burden on any individual. More people involved means that the task is more likely to get done—because the work is shared, and because there exists a diverse set of skills. More people mean fewer problems will emerge, because there are more experiences and more ideas to offer to the plans. Being involved in the community on a part-time basis is part of the American Way.

Summary

The principles of the American Way are firm and perfect; however the details will need adjusting as circumstances change. There are ways to do this, and ways not to do this.

Here I have offered a brief picture of how changes are made in America. These include: 1. Evolution, 2. Persuasion, 3. Peaceful communication, 4. Work with businesses, 5. Discussion with many people, and 6. All the community involved part-time.

PART VII
Conclusion

Conclusion

There is an American Way.

The American Way is a combination of many things. These elements include: freedom to run your own life; government run by the people; freedom of speech; freedom to be religious; freedom of choice; free market economy; limited government; rule of law; laws created by the people; justice administered by the people; opportunity for all; equality for all under the law; equality in rights of participation in the government; code of ethics; community spirit; ingenuity; and changes through evolution. These are but a few elements of the American Way.

America is successful in so many areas because of the American Way. In order to ensure our success for the future, we must teach the American Way to others.

The American Way is not a simple formula. It cannot be learned in just a day. Even during the founding of this country, the great founders took time to develop America. Colonials lived the American Way, refining the principles over decades of practice. The most brilliant minds of the time discussed the concepts, usually in evening discussions, and often in discussions that lasted for days. Those who crafted the great documents of our history did not just pull them from the air, rather they studied history, and they discussed political philosophy, before setting pen to paper.

Thus, the American Way is not entirely simple. It takes time to really learn and to really understand all of the facets.

We do not want the keys to America's greatness to be hidden. We want all Americans to know the keys. In fact, we want to share the keys to our greatness with all of the world. That, too, is part of the American Way. (But, it should be noted, that it takes years for any country which is new to the concepts of our nation to finally grasp them and really live them.)

Note that I have traveled. I state this to emphasize what I have seen, for my traveling has helped me to understand America. Note that in all my travels, I was as a regular man on the street. There were never any fancy tours or rich hotels. I lived simply, I talked with the people, and I lived as one of them.

I have been to Communist countries and to third world nations. I have seen military rule and I've seen fear among the people. I have seen areas of no plumbing, no electricity, and extreme poverty. I have seen areas where safety in daily life is abysmal.

America is none of these things. America is free, safe, and prosperous.

I have seen much of America as well. I've spent time in many states. I've seen different areas—from city to country, from liberal to conservative, from prosperous to stagnant. I've taught at inner city schools and seen the inner city life up close. I've also seen the wealthy areas, learning how they became so prosperous. I've spent time with the artists in the coffee shops, and with the people of various lifestyles in the larger cities. I have also lived among the simple, country folk of this nation.

I have been involved in community projects and with community groups. I've seen the great things that civic clubs have done for their communities. I've been involved in government—from local to national, and even a few times to our nation's capitol.

I have seen individuals start a business and become successful. I have spent time in some of our greatest parks. I have seen healthy communities. I have seen Americans living out the ideals—the great ideals that many cynics think can't really exist.

Yes, I know about America.

I know what America is, and what America is not. America is a great place. We must understand what makes America so wonderful, what makes it so different from all other nations. We must preserve all aspects of the American Way so that our blessings can continue.

There is an American Way. It is broad, and very inclusive, but there is an American Way. As broad as the American Way is, there are definite limits.

We do not care what your background is. We do not ask your race, sex, or religion. However, we do ask one question: Do you believe in the American Way?

America is like a club. We are probably the most open club around, but, as with all clubs, we do have criteria. We have only one question for you: Do you believe in the American Way?

We are the most polite, the most tolerant, the most charitable people on earth, but we do have limits. Again, do you believe in the American Way?

Being an American is a privilege. It is not a right merely because you exist. We've been letting people come here who don't deserve this privilege. We've been letting disruptive anti-Americans disrupt our communities long enough. We've been politely tolerant—but that must stop.

I've got only one question: Do you believe in the American Way? If you don't believe in the American Way, then you are not allowed to have any of the privileges of being an American. We are open-minded and tolerant, more so than any other nation, yet there are limits.

If a citizen does not believe in the American Way, then we won't give his arguments any serious consideration, for his ideas have no place in America. If an immigrant does not believe in the American Way, then we should not let him in. We are under no obligation to do so.

Why do immigrants come here? Why are other nations jealous of us? Obviously, we have something that works. If other countries worked as well as America does, then few people from other countries would leave their homes for America. If the people of other countries were as prosperous as the people in America, then the people of those nations wouldn't leave home and they wouldn't be jealous.

To repeat: we obviously have something that works. So, why should we change something if it works? Why tinker with success? We should hold onto the principles of our success, and we should teach those principles to other countries. Don't tinker with success—keep it and pass it on.

Some people are trying to take us down roads that are bad for America. Too many people want us to be like other countries. I know the end result. You don't need to be a prophet or an academic scholar to figure this out. Anyone who has seen the results first hand can see the danger. I don't want American life to become like life in those other countries. I have seen these other countries—and they are disasters.

Again I refer to my travels. I talk of my travels to emphasize what I have seen. I've seen it, and I don't want it.

Other countries limit speech, and they limit the press. Other countries limit an individual's freedom to live as he wants, and limit his ability to become successful. In other countries, the government harms those that don't agree with the leaders. In many countries, the government forces one religion as the only religion, and destroys all others.

Other countries have a culture of no ethics, where theft is a way of life. Many countries have definite class systems, and if you are in the lower class there is no chance for personal success, or even a role in the government.

I've seen shortage of goods, dangerous daily life, and broken trains. I've seen military rule and oppressive governments. I've seen areas of no plumbing, unreliable energy, and questionable food safety. I've seen true poverty, real government oppression, and deeply believed class systems. I've seen areas where concepts such as trust, fairness, and equality are as impossible as walking on the sun. I've seen all these things...and I don't want them.

Don't tell me that you are mistreated or oppressed here in America. Don't talk to me about being treated unequally or being treated unfairly. I've seen other countries. I've read my history. I know better.

To repeat: I have seen these other countries. Their way is not the American Way—and it shows. I do not want our nation to become like those. Instead, I want to preserve our successful methods, and teach it to all immigrants and all new generations. I even want those other less successful nations to become like ours.

There *is* an American Way. The American Way has been very successful for hundreds of years. Do not tinker with success. Instead, we must *understand* the American Way. We must continue to teach it and must continue to live it. We must fight each and every day in order to preserve it.

We must always work to preserve the American Way.

Always.

APPENDIX A

Understanding America

✦

Suggested Reading of Books and Websites

1. The US Constitution
Website: http://www.usconstitution.net/const.html

2. The Declaration of Independence
Website: http://www.usconstitution.net/declar.html

3. The Pledge of Allegiance explained
Website: http://home.att.net/~poofcatt/july.html
(note: you do not need the plug-in. Hit cancel and read)

4. Colonial Hall—Biographies of Founding Fathers
website: http://www.colonialhall.com/index.asp

5. Book of historical documents, speeches, and essays:
The Patriots Handbook: A Citizenship Primer for a New Generation of Americans,
by George Grant, Ph.D., 1996 Cumberland House

6. Book of good behavior and being part of the community:
The Good Citizen's Handbook: A Guide to Proper Behavior
by Jennifer McKnight-Trontz, 2001 Chronicle Books

7. Ethical Codes of the West:
www.phantomranch.net/bwestern/creeds.htm

APPENDIX B

Civic groups and volunteer organizations

Listed alphabetically

Adopt-a-Highway	www.adoptahighway.com
Big Brother/Big Sister	www.bbbsa.org
Boys and Girls and Clubs of America	www.bgca.org
Boy Scouts	www.scouting.org
Child Welfare League (mentoring)	www.cwla.org
City Cares	www.citycares.org
Corp. for National Community Service	www.nationalservice.org

Incl. Senior Corps, AmeriCorps, and Learn and Serve America

Do Something	www.dosomething.org
Eagles	www.foe.com
Elks	www.elks.org
Four H	www.national4-hheadquarters.gov/4h_map.htm
Girl Scouts	www.girlscouts.org
Grange	www.nationalgrange.org
Jaycees	www.usjaycees.org/main.htm
Junior Leagues (women of all ages)	www.ajli.org/home.html
Keep America Beautiful	www.kab.org
Kiwanis	www.kiwanis.org

Lions	www.lionsclubs.org/EN/index.shtml
Mentoring.org	www.mentoring.org
Network for Good	www.networkforgood.org
Oddfellows	www.ioof.org
(so named because helping others was thought "odd")	
Optimist	www.optimist.org
Red Cross	www.redcross.org
Round Table	www.roundtableintl.org/index.shtml
Rotary Club	www.rotary.org
Salvation Army	www.salvationarmyusa.org
Sertoma (service to mankind)	www.sertoma.org
USA Freedom Corps	www.usafreedomcorps.gov
Volunteer.gov	www.volunteer.gov/gov
Volunteer Match	www.volunteermatch.org
Volunteer.org	www.1-800-volunteer.org
We Prevent (Crime Prevention)	www.weprevent.org
YMCA	www.ymca.net

APPENDIX C

Groups to join to help preserve the American Way

KEY ACTIVIST GROUPS
Those involved in many projects

e-minutemen	www.eminutemen.com
ACLJ	www.aclj.org
The 60 Second Activist	www.SixtySecondActivist.com/
Citizens Lobby	www.citizenslobby.com/
Family Policy Network	www.familypolicy.net
Conservative Education Forum	www.truthusa.com/cindy.html
Heritage	www.heritage.org/issues/
Institute for Justice	www.IJ.org/index.shtml

ACTIVIST GROUPS BY ISSUE TOPIC

Boy Scouts—defending Boy Scouts

eminutmen	www.eminutemen.com/boyscoutspage1.htm
Defending Scouting	www.defendscouting.com

Census Reform

eminutemen	www.eminutemen.com/Census%20Main.htm

Crime Prevention and Community Watch

National Crime Prevention Council	www.ncpc.org/
We Prevent	www.weprevent.org
Crime Prevent Coalition	www.crimepreventcoalition.org/
Crime Prevention Resources	www.crimeprevent.com/
Prevent Crime (Michigan)	www.preventcrime.net
Texas Crime Prevention Association	www.tcpa.org

Community Watch—Orange County, CA, but good info for all areas
    www.co.orange.nc.us/sheriff/community_watch.htm
Community Watch—Huntsville, AL—but good info for all areas
    www.hsvcommunitywatch.com/about.htm
National Neighborhood Watch Institute (training materials, signs)
    www.nnwi.org/index.html

Education and Parenting:

eminutmen	www.eminutemen.com/eduction2.htm
Center for Education Reform	www.edreform.com
Conservative Educators Caucus	www.ceccentral.org
Save Our Schools Network	www.3dresearch.com/hoge/

Information site on education	www.e-files.org
Character in Education	www.cyi-stars.org/federalist/federalist.htm
How Education in your state is doing	www.heritage.org/reportcards/
Parents Television Council	www.parentstv.org

Election Reform

eminutemen	www.eminutemen.com/ElectionReformProject.htm
Vote Fraud	http://votefraud.org/

Energy issues

eminutmen	www.eminutemen.com/energy.htm

English as Official Language

US English Inc.	http://www.us-english.org/inc/

Immigration

e-minutemen	www.eminutemen.com/immigration.htm
California Coalition	www.ccir.net
American Patrol	www.americanpatrol.com
Citizens Lobby	www.citizenslobby.com/
Federation for Immigration Reform	www.fair.org

Judicial Reform and Judges who know American Way

eminutemen	www.eminutemen.com/judicaReform.htm
Free Congress	www.freecongress.org/
Federalist Society	www.fed-soc.org

Lawsuits *for* America—protecting the American Way

These are legal groups fighting for specific issues in the courtroom. They are on our side—the side of America. They will protect your freedoms and your rights.

ACLJ	www.aclj.org
Alliance Defend Fund	www.alliancedefensefund.org
Institute for Justice	www.IJ.org/index.shtml
Save California	www.savecalifornia.com/

Legal reform—stop abusive lawsuits

Lawsuit Abuse Tax	www.lawsuitabusetax.com
Citizens Against Lawsuit Abuse	www.cala.com
American Tort Reform Assoc.	www.ATRA.org/

Petitions

eminutemen	www.eminutemen.com/petitions.htm
Conservative petitions	www.conservativepetitions.com
Petition On-line	www.PetitionOnline.com/petition.html
Liberty petitions	www.libertypetitions.com

Pledge of Allegiance

eminutemen	www.eminutemen.com/pledgeofAllegiance.htm

Privacy

Defend your privacy	http://defendyourprivacy.com/
Privacy rights	http://www.privacyrights.org

Property Rights—stopping eminent domain abuse

Institute for Justice	www.IJ.org
landrights.org	www.landrights.org/
eminutemen	www.eminutemen.com/privateproperty.htm

Religious Freedom

eminutmen	www.eminutemen.com/religion.htm
Faith and Action	www.faithandaction.org

Second Amendment Rights

NRA	www.nra.org
Gun Owners of America	www.gunowners.org/
Second Amendment Foundation	www.saf.org/
Keep and Bear Arms	www.keepandbeararms.com/
Concealed Carry, Inc.	www.concealcarry.org/
Guns Save Lives	www.gunssavelives.com/
Citizens Committee to Keep & Bear Arms	www.ccrkba.org/
Second Amendment Sisters	www.sas-aim.org/
Armed Females of America	www.armedfemalesofamerica.com
Jews For The Preservation Of Firearms	www.jpfo.org/
Seniors United Supporting the Second Amendment	www.sussa.org
Doctors for Responsible Gun Ownership	www.claremont.org/projects/doctors/index.html

Taxes

Americans for Tax Reform	www.atr.org/main.htm
eminutemen	www.eminutemen.com/taxes.htm

APPENDIX D

Suggested laws to ensure the American Way

Whenever new people threaten our way of life, whenever the government finds new ways of taking our liberties, then we must write laws and Constitutional Amendments to preserve the American Way.

This is a set of laws that Americans should enact in their communities. Most of these laws have come from concerned, activist citizens throughout our nation.

We, the People, must push for these laws at every level—city, state, and federal. Most of these laws are connected to the principles of Freedom and Self-Government.

Many issues in government today arise from the fact that many in government think they are more powerful than the people. We must remember that those who work in the government are our employees. They are merely our agents. The great majority of these suggested laws are to address the balance of power, limiting government and putting the people back in control.

Other problems have come about because a minority group forces its views on the majority. The American Way regarding the majority-minority relationship means two things:
1) The majority gets to decide all issues, not the minority. 2) We allow the minority to exist, without persecuting them.

However, too many minorities are pushing their way against the majority. In many issues, there exists a minority of 10% or less trying to stop something which a majority of 70% or more of the people want. (The other 20% are undecided on many issues). The majority must be allowed to live their lives and run their communities as they want, without interference from the minority. Thus, some of the laws suggested here ensure just that.

We, the People, must get these laws passed. It is up to good Americans like you to work hard to push for these laws.

It is important to emphasize that we must get these laws passed ourselves. When the government is not getting these laws passed, then we must do it. We must put the initiatives on the ballots. We must replace representatives with other representatives. We will run for office ourselves.

We are the government. We are the community. We decide.

Do the work required to make our views part of the law. Get your community involved. Explain the issue and explain the solution. Get your fellow citizens to write their representatives, to sign petitions, to get initiatives on the ballot, and to vote in the American Way.

We will do all these things so that laws of the American Way can indeed be made permanent. We will do all these things in order to preserve our freedoms, to limit the government, and return to living the American Way.

Suggested laws Americans should pass—in brief

A. <u>The People and the Representatives</u>

1. Citizens should be able to sign up to receive monthly updates from each of their representatives.

2. Referendums: it must be easy for the people of every jurisdiction (city, county, state, and federal) to put propositions on the ballots.

3. All salary increases for members of any legislature must be voted on directly by the people.

4. A representative elected to office cannot switch his party identification while in office.

5. The term "filibuster" must return to its original meaning—an act of physical endurance.

6. Changes in procedures in Congress must be voted on by the people.

7. If a state representative leaves his state during a vote and refuses to come back, then he will lose his job immediately.

8. Politicians who slander their opponents should be charged in the courts with slander and a hate crime.

9. No retirement pay for government employees or representatives until they reach the age of 65.

B. <u>Finances, Budgets, and Taxes</u>

10. Require all public high schools to teach a one year course in finances.

11. Budgets must be made accessible to all citizens every year, primarily through a website and through summaries mailed to each home.

12. All tax increases must be voted on directly by the people.

13. The Income Tax should be abolished, through an Amendment to the Constitution

14. No gift or inheritance can be taxed. These laws must be made permanent, preferably through an Amendment to the Constitution.

C. <u>Judges</u>

15. All Judges of higher courts must be elected directly by the people, not appointed or voted into office by legislatures. In addition, all Judges must be re-elected every few years, no longer serving for life.

D. <u>Freedom of Religion</u>

16. All matters regarding religion and government must be put to a direct vote by the people on a November ballot. Neither legislatures nor judges will be allowed to rule on such important matters.

17. No religious item (such as plaque or prayer) currently in place can be removed by a minority view. Instead, if the minority view finds it offensive, he can only add to that. It will be illegal to take away any religious item; we can only add religious displays, not subtract.

E. <u>Melting pot and Civics education</u>

18. English must be made the official language.

19. All High School students must take one semester of civics.

20. Require all immigrants to take an on-going, multi-level civics course as long as they live in this country. Not attending the classes or failing any portion of the class multiple times will disqualify extension of their visa. The course in total should be several hundred hours over a 3–5 year period.

21. Race can no longer be asked. No government agency, school, or business can ask about race on official forms.

22. All illegal immigrants must be sent back immediately.

23. Anyone who offers benefits for illegal immigrants, and anyone who hires illegal immigrants, must be tried in the courts for aiding and abetting a known criminal.

F. <u>Eminent Domain and Private Property</u>

24. Eminent Domain laws must be rewritten to specifically state what uses can and cannot be considered eminent domain.

25. Eminent Domain laws must state that the government must try other solutions before seeking to claim property for eminent domain. The government must prove to the landowners that all other options have been considered.

26. Eminent Domain laws must mandate that property can be taken only if the property owner agrees, or if the people approve of it through a direct vote on a November ballot.

G. <u>Right to Privacy</u>

27. Government is not allowed to sell personal information.

28. Only those with authority may have access to personal information or history.

29. Create a Constitutional Amendment for Right to Privacy.

30. Census reform: no questions on income, work, home, or race.

31. We must write laws stating very specifically where the boundaries of privacy are for business and governments, on many specific issues.

SUGGESTED LAWS AMERICANS SHOULD PASS—IN DETAIL

A. <u>The People and the Representatives</u>

1. <u>Citizens should be able to sign up to receive monthly updates from each of their representatives</u>.

These monthly updates can be sent through the e-mail. There will be two sections: future and past. The future section will detail all the new bills, procedures, judges and so forth being discussed and voted on in the upcoming month. Bills will be listed as bill number and brief description.

The past section will detail the representatives' specific votes and actions. This should be a list of bills (bill number and one sentence reminder of what it was) and how he voted. This must also be done for all votes on new procedures, judges and so forth.

Along with the list of yes or no for each vote, the representative should also explain the reason why he voted the way he did, one paragraph minimum per item.

<u>Reason</u>:

Representatives act as our agents, they are our employees. All managers must communicate with all their employees. If not, employees often don't do their job, and even take money for themselves without producing. The same holds true for government. The representatives must send their bosses (the people) regular letters explaining what they have done recently. In business, often contracted employees send e-mail updates once a week or once a month. The same should exist for our employees in the legislatures.

By doing this over e-mail, there is essentially no cost. By making it an option to sign up for it, then only those who want it will receive it, and there will be no invasion of privacy.

Listing future items for discussion will let the people know what the business in government currently is. If anyone has a passionate view about an item, he can let his representative know right away, before the vote.

Listing past items and how he voted is equally as important. We must see what our employees are doing. A quick scan down the list and we can see if his judgment seems to agree with our own. If not, then we investigate. Further, by explaining why he voted the way he did on each issue, then anyone who questions the decision can learn why. This will answer most questions.

If the people do not like the voting decision of the representative, they have a right to tell him so. If his voting decisions and actions are too often in contrast with the people, then they also have the right to replace him in the next election.

Because we have so many representatives, just as a business owner has many employees, then we need communication with all of them. Getting a monthly report from each representative will greatly benefit the people.

2. <u>The people of every jurisdiction—city, county, state, and federal—must have an easy method to get propositions on the ballot.</u>

These propositions will get on the ballot based on a number of signatures (always a certain percentage of the population of the jurisdiction), then they will be voted on directly by the people.

Reason:

In America, the people run the government. The only reason we have representatives is because it is not practical for citizens to be in all the legislatures on a daily basis. However, the government is still run by the people.

If the representatives are not doing their job, if there are needs that the people must have addressed, and yet the legislature is not addressing these issues, then, the people have the full right to propose a law directly and have the people vote on that law directly.

As it currently exists, only some areas have the option of referendums. Furthermore, many states allow referendums only if the legislature—not even the people—vote to have a proposition on the ballot. Instead, what should happen is that the people have the right to propose propositions at any time they choose.

Also, as it currently exists, states may have referendum options, but not cities or counties. Again, people of all jurisdictions must have the right to get referendums on ballots. It is the people's right, because the people run the government.

3. <u>All salary increases for members of any legislature must be voted on directly by the people.</u>

Reason:

As long as legislatures can vote themselves pay increases, there is nothing to stop them from making them wealthy through stealing from the people.

4. <u>A representative elected to office cannot switch his party identification while in</u> <u>office</u>.

If he switches parties, then he will lose his office and a new election will be held the following November. The majority-minority party designations will not change if party members switch.

<u>Reason</u>:

This representative was elected based on that party. As an employee of the people, he must represent himself as identified to the people on that ballot through the remainder of his term. Further, his switching has no relation to what the people elected him to. This is equivalent to lying on your job application, and therefore he should lose his job. Also, because his switching parties is no relation to the people who hired him, then designations of majority party is not affected. (This issue comes from the Jim Jeffords case)

5. <u>The term "filibuster" must return to its original meaning—an act of physical</u> <u>endurance</u>. A man who filibusters must physically stand and talk day and night until he quits or falls down. It is wrong to say that a certain number of voting officials is equivalent to a filibuster.

<u>Reason</u>:

Little did the public know that some time ago Congress let people "filibuster" without actually doing it. This is akin to winning a touchdown without actually playing football, or getting a pilot's license without getting into a plane. You have to do the work to get it.

This rule has prevented good judges from being appointed, and good laws from being passed. The terrible thing is that the Democrats don't have to lift a finger to cause this trouble. Therefore, the term filibuster must be physical endurance, and not just a voting block.

6. <u>Changes in voting procedures and balance of power in Congress must be voted</u> <u>on by the people</u>.

<u>Reason</u>:

This will prevent things like that "filibuster" replacement from ever happening again.

7. <u>If a state representative leaves the floor during a vote, particularly if he leaves his state, then he will be called back. If he refuses to come back, then he will lose his job immediately.</u>

The Governor of the state will be allowed to name replacements, from any party he chooses, for each representative who fails to show for work.

<u>Reason</u>:

This is from the Texas redistricting nightmare. The current law requires a certain number of representatives to vote on the law. However, all the Democrats left the state, and therefore, by law, no vote can be taken. The Democrats have done this twice now, and think they are cute. The people, however, know better.

Any regular person who doesn't show up for work will be fired on the spot. The representatives are our employees—we hired them, and we pay their salaries. For them to not show up for work, for a month at a time, is outrageous. If they were employees at any company, they'd all be fired. Therefore, since they are employees of the people, they should get the same treatment: fire them immediately and hire new ones.

8. <u>Elected politicians who slander their opponents should be charged with both slander and a hate crime.</u>

They should be judged in a court. Slander is shown to exist when the statements can be proven false. Hate crime should be applied because the purpose of their slander is to destroy the career of someone they hate. Punishments for slander must include fines and public apologies. If slander is proven, then the politician must pay the full legal bills for both parties.

<u>Reason</u>:

Democrats slander constantly. The name calling is tiresome to all Americans, and does not provide discussion. Their slander is so horrible, comparing Republicans to Hitler, implying they are racist, and suggesting they condone violence. If we charge them, then their statements will be shown to be false, and they must make a public apology—along with financial costs. Perhaps this will reduce some of the Democrat's slander and get us to real discussions.

9. <u>No retirement pay for government employees until 65.</u>

No government person shall get any retirement until after he is 65, or is no longer physically able to work. This includes US Senators.

Reason:

As it currently exists, many representatives get a retirement package. This is no ordinary retirement package, for they get that retirement pay for the rest of their lives. U.S. Senators, for example, only have to serve one term of office, then get a free salary forever.

This is fundamentally wrong, on many levels. The people are the ones who pay for government, therefore excess government cost is an insult to the people.

They need to work, just like the rest of us. We paid them for a job. They did the job. Now that they've left, they must work another job. We don't have to pay them anymore.

Furthermore, these senators are able to work, and, because they were senator, they will be in high demand for lots of jobs. Therefore, there is no reason to give these Senators our money for not working.

B. Taxes, Budgets, and Finances

10. Require all public high schools to teach a one year course in finances.

This course must include: household finances; loans and credit cards; stocks; business costs; government spending; effects of lawsuits; retirement; and health care. All students must practice using chips, fake money, or on paper.

Reason:

America has many financial troubles. We cannot expect Americans to make financially good decisions unless they have a strong understanding of practical financial issues.

This affects the family, such as with personal debt, and the effects of bad judgments. This also effects the government—as spending and deficits grow out of control. The only way to remedy these problems is for all Americans to take a course in practical, financial concepts and skills.

11. Budgets must be made accessible to all citizens every year.

Budgets must be posted on a website. These budgets must be in full detail, and easily accessible. Further, summaries of the budgets should be mailed to homes every year.

Reason:

We need to see where our money is going. It is our money, not theirs. They always demand more. Well, let's see exactly what they are doing. This will make them accountable.

12. <u>All tax increases must be voted on by the people.</u>

This includes income tax increases, sales tax increases, and property tax increases. Further note that the word "property tax" must be stated, and not "ad velorem", which is a term few people know.

Reason:

The money in the public treasuries belongs to the people. It is never the government's money. Rather, the people agree to share the cost of services which benefit the entire community.

Since the people pay, the people must decide if the extra expense is worth it or not. The burden of proof for extra money is put on the government—the government must convince the people that the government has done all it can to keep costs down, and that this increase is realistic. The people then vote on it.

All good business managers know this. Managers are always checking on expenses. People request expenses for things, but whoever pays the bills must approve of the expenses. Otherwise, people just spend, spend, spend. And so it has been in government at all levels.

13. <u>The Income Tax should be abolished</u>.

All federal income tax and state income tax should be declared unconstitutional. We can do this through an Amendment to the Constitution.

Reason:

The income tax should never have been passed in the first place. Since the days of the creation of the income tax, government has grown to gargantuan size, and the burden on the people has grown to oppressive levels. The situation has become like the kings of old stealing from the peasants, when, in fact, the government should be limited and should be working for us.

Like the old issue of prohibition, we can repeal the income tax with another amendment.

14. <u>No gift can be taxed. No inheritance can be taxed. These laws must be made permanent, preferably through an Amendment to the Constitution.</u>

Reason:

Even if we concede to the point that some of your income needs to be shared with the community (which I don't agree), at least that is income you earned. Gifts and inheritance are not the same as income. A gift, by definition, was something given to you. Furthermore, why should the government be involved at all? These are private affairs.

A gift is not income—you didn't pay for the gift. Thus, many people who get gifts often have to sell them just to pay for the taxes. It is in this way that many family farms and family businesses have been lost to the family—the rightful owners. One man works hard all his life, and he gives the fruits of his labors to his family when he is gone. Yet, they didn't get the gift at all. They had to sell it in order to pay taxes.

Furthermore, the person who did the giving spent the same amount of money on the gift regardless of who gets it. It does no good for him to give this wonderful gift, and then the receiver is not allowed to use it. There is no pleasure for the giver, or the receiver. The only pleasure goes to the government, as it gets rewarded for its theft.

Inheritance is similar. A man worked hard all his life for his property, his money, his farm, or his business. He should do what he wants with it. Furthermore, he was already taxed on these throughout his life. Why should there be a double tax on the same items after his death?

Many people who inherit things cannot afford them. They have to sell them off just to pay for the taxes. This is not right.

Like gifts, inheritance was not earned income. It is not as if the person had income to afford this inheritance item, plus more. No, the person got the item as a gift—at no cost. Therefore, since no money was spent, there is no money to give to anyone—including to the government.

These must be made illegal.

Furthermore, these must be made permanent. Few people realize that even when a new tax plan is passed with these items, the particulars don't start for a few years, and then they only last a few years. It all resets. It resets in favor of the government, not in favor of the people. It resets to the government being able to take all the money they want. Thus, these tax laws must be made permanent, without expiration.

To really prevent the greedy government from stealing, it is best if we have Constitutional Amendments. Once passed, then no one can talk of taking from the people through gifts or inheritance again.

C. Judges

15. <u>Federal judges must be elected directly by the people, and must be re-elected every few years</u>. Judges will no longer hold positions for life. The U.S. Supreme Court will be the only exception.

<u>Reason</u>:

Judges throughout the land have taken powers beyond their authority. Many, many judges, at all levels, think it is their right to make laws and to change laws they don't like. This is not true. Their only legal power is to apply the laws that exist, not make new ones. Judges who reach beyond their legal authority must be replaced.

Many judges are also un-American. They allow frivolous lawsuits, they allow lawsuits against America, and they stop the desires of the people. These judges are not representative of the people, they are not representative of America, and should have no place as judges in our courts.

Several judicial positions are appointed for life. This is most unusual—even the President cannot serve for life. There are good reasons for having terms of office, rather than lifetime positions. Only with terms and re-elections can we get bad people out of government. Therefore, judges at all levels (except US Supreme Court) must reapply for their job every few years, for then we can terminate the jobs of the bad judges.

Judges should also be elected directly by the people. The people dislike what the judges do, but have little power, for most judges are appointed or confirmed through legislatures. Therefore, judges should be elected directly by the people.

Judges today do not know their proper role. Therefore, the people must write laws and add amendments to limit their role. All judges, particularly federal judges and state supreme court justices, must be elected directly by the people, and must apply for their job (run for re-election) every few years.

D. <u>Freedom of Religion</u>

<u>16. All matters regarding religion and government must be put to a direct vote by the people on a November ballot. Neither legislatures nor judges will be allowed to rule on such important matters.</u>

Example on a ballot: "Should the Ten Commandments plaque in the City Park be kept or be removed?" Choice on ballot: "Keep plaque/Remove plaque"

<u>Reason:</u>

The issues of religious freedom are too important to be decided by a mere court, they must be decided by the people of each community directly.

Furthermore, most judges are traitors—their actions clearly go against the Constitution. They are unfit to judge anything. Therefore, the people must take back the role of judging these matters directly.

Remember how America should work in these matters: The people rule themselves. They are free to have religious beliefs as they wish. They are free to run the government and community issues as they wish. No one has a right to stop the majority from doing what they wish.

Further, if the majority of the community believes in a particular religion, and they want public displays, then no one is allowed to prevent them. This is not just for Christianity, but for any religion—if a particular town is majority Buddhist, then they have a right to put Buddhist plaques and have Buddhist prayers if they like.

Currently, there are pushy minorities who want to stop the people from enjoying life. The judges are traitors, and they agree with the minority view. To bypass this, we *must* put these important issues directly to the people.

When the people are allowed to vote on the issue directly, then it will be clear that the great majority of the community want those plaques and prayers to stay. There will be no confusion—the people will vote for these religious items to stay. Once the vote to remove a plaque has been turned down by the people, then that is the end of it.

We must specify the item go on the November ballot so that all people vote. Again, tricky traitors like to hold special voting times for un-American issues, which most people are unaware of, and hence those votes passed in favor of traitors are really frauds. To prevent this, all issues must be put on the November ballot.

17. No religious item (plaque or prayer) currently in place can be removed by a minority view. Instead, if the minority view finds it offensive, he can only add to that. It will be illegal to take away any religious item; we can only add religious displays, not subtract.

For example, instead of removing the Ten Commandments plaque, add a religious plaque of their particular religion next to it. Thus, their beliefs will be represented as well as the ones currently displayed. For example, instead of denying Christians their prayers at sporting events, add another prayer from another faith to the traditional beginning of those events in the community.

Reason:

The people are allowed to live as they want. This is a key principle of the American Way. If the majority has a certain belief, then they should be allowed to have that.

If a minority view finds offense in that, first they should ignore it—they are the minority and really have no say on any issue. Yet, too often today the minority dictates their views to the majority. We cannot let this go on.

Most Americans would allow the other view to have equal visibility and equal time. What we cannot allow is for our way of life and our beliefs to be removed.

This concept is already established within the First Amendment regarding Freedom of Religion. However, it seems we must make this more specific today: we can only add religious displays, not subtract.

Thus, with this law, people who don't agree with certain faiths will always be allowed to add their views—that means adding their plaques, their prayers, and their beliefs. Yet the minority will always be *forbidden* from taking away anything of other beliefs—they will no longer be able to remove plaques, stop prayers, or prevent religious displays. This is particularly important because the beliefs being taken away are the beliefs of the great majority of every community. This practice must be specified as illegal.

E. <u>Melting Pot and Civics Education</u>

18. <u>English must be made the official language</u>

English must be made the official language, first of every state, then of the United States. This is best done as a Constitutional Amendment to each state constitution and to the U.S. Constitution

<u>Reason:</u>

The purpose of language is to communicate. Without a common language, then we cannot work together or live together effectively.

English has been our language, and has been our language for many years. However, without making it the official language, we have become more diverse in language over the years. Immigrants refuse to learn English, and governments cater to the immigrants by printing documents and holding debates in other languages. This must stop.

It should be noted that throughout our history good people have tried to get this as the official language. For various reasons, this has not yet been successful. However, I do not know why this is such a difficult law to pass.

19. <u>Require all public high schools to teach a one semester course in civics</u>

<u>Reason:</u>

In order to preserve the American Way, we must teach it to each generation. Civics is a multifaceted subject, and is vital to everything in our country. In the past, civics was taught, yet today very few schools do. This is not by accident, for communists and socialists have taken over the educational system in this country long ago. Their system is not the American Way, and after many years of no civics classes, we can clearly see the damaging consequences in this country. Therefore, we must force the schools to teach civics.

20. <u>Require all immigrants to take an on-going multi-level civics course as long as they live in this country. Not attending the classes or failing any level will disqualify extension of their visa. The course in total should be several hundred hours over a 5 year period.</u>

These classes could be run through private sector schools, through businesses, or through the government. Holding classes one day a week for most weeks of the year would be convenient and realistic, as well as a good pace to learn about America.

Funding for these classes can come from the immigrants themselves or through the government (the people). As this falls into the realm of public education, this may be a realistic item for the people to help pay for.

Making this class mandatory will make sure that immigrants will go regularly. Making it a weekly class from the very first week the immigrants arrive in America will force immigrants to learn about America and start to live the American Way.

Reason:

Immigrants today are not required to know anything about America. As more people come from other countries, but know not of the American Way, the American Way has become less known, more diluted, and is more at risk. Furthermore, many immigrants today, unlike most immigrants of the past, see America as a place to steal from. Ethics, manners, and morals do not seem to phase these modern immigrants. This lack of ethics is not the American Way. Hence, all immigrants must learn the American Way. They must continue to learn it and live it while they are here.

All Americans must learn the American Way, whether born here or immigrated here. The subject has so many parts, and each concept is important, that it takes time to learn the total of the American Way. Citizens born in America go through approximately 800 hours of civics in their schooling—including English, History, and Civics. We should expect at least that much, if not more, from immigrants.

Furthermore, since it takes time to learn, having the classes one day a week for most of the year, over 3–5 years, provides an excellent way for the immigrants to learn about America over time.

21. No government agency, school, or business can ask about race on applications or official forms. Alternate law: until the above law is passed, the term "American" must be the first choice of those choices listed.

Reason:

America is an idea. It is a set of principles. It is not about race. We are a melting pot, where there is no one race. All ethnic backgrounds are blended together through marriages over many years, until there is only one ethnicity: American.

Furthermore, our history is one of granting more freedoms and rights to people of different ethnic backgrounds throughout the years. Therefore it is wrong on every level to ask Americans to choose a race. This is not egalitarian. It is only divisive.

These questions should never be asked.

The real reason behind those questions is so that liberals can get more money. There exists an entire job structure based on race. The money doesn't help the individuals that the money was intended for, it just feeds a bureaucracy. That is, the money for these "programs" pays for the liberals' salaries in these artificial bureaucracies. That is the only reason why certain Americans want to keep those race questions.

Nevertheless, these questions are un-American in every respect and should be made illegal. To ensure this, it is best to have an Amendment to the Constitution.

22. <u>All illegal immigrants must be sent back immediately.</u>

There is a proper procedure for everything, including the privilege of coming into America. Those who are illegal, by whatever term, for whatever reasons, must be sent back. There is no exception.

<u>Reason:</u>

Immigrants who came here illegally have committed a crime. There is no doubt about that. It is the same as a doctor practicing without a license. The law is clear and not debatable.

Therefore, all illegal immigrants must be taken up immediately and sent back to their native country.

23. <u>Anyone who offers benefits for illegal immigrants, and anyone who hires illegal immigrants, must be tried in the courts for aiding and abetting a criminal.</u>

<u>Reasons:</u>

Assisting and protecting a criminal is in itself a criminal offense. Anyone who assists and protects a thief, a murderer, or a rapist is himself committing a crime.

By definition, illegal immigrants have committed a crime. Therefore, anyone who supports them, who tries to help them, is himself committing a crime.

Therefore, anyone who talks publicly about supporting these illegal immigrants must be watched. Speaking is not a crime, but actions can be, and most people who speak publicly will in fact follow through with their proposed actions. Anyone who talks publicly about committing a crime—such as helping illegals—should be watched.

Furthermore, if a man assists illegal immigrants, he has not only committed a crime, but his earlier public statements are in fact confessions of this crime which can be used against him. He must be tried in the courts, by the people, for aiding and abetting a criminal.

Furthermore, the number of illegal immigrants he talks of helping makes a greater number of counts against him. Aiding one criminal makes one count, aiding a thousand immigrants makes a thousand counts.

Some of the specific aiding and abetting crimes for aiding illegal immigrants include the following: 1) Offering to give illegals amnesty. 2) Offering to give illegals social services, such as health care. 3) Refusing to deport known illegal immigrants. 4) Offering drivers licenses to illegal immigrants.

Those who hire illegals are also guilty of aiding and abetting criminals.

The obviousness is clear: these immigrants are committing a crime by being here illegally. Therefore it is wrong to pay them and protect them.

F. <u>Eminent Domain and Private Property</u>

24. <u>Eminent Domain laws must be rewritten to specifically state what uses can and cannot be considered eminent domain.</u>

Property can be taken for eminent domain for purposes of: schools, utilities, and transportation. Property cannot be taken for purposes of private businesses or redevelopment.

<u>Reasons</u>:

In recent decades governments at all levels have abused the eminent domain prerogative. One of the greatest satisfactions in a man's life is to own property. A man works hard to attain this property, and often the family tries to keep it in the family for generations. Taking a man's property for public use should never be done lightly.

25. <u>Eminent Domain laws must state that the government must try other solutions before seeking to claim property for eminent domain. The government must prove that all other options have been considered.</u>

Alternate solutions include the following: using vacant and bankrupt business sites; using reclaimed land such as from mining; claiming property destroyed after a natural disaster; and building high speed rail lines along existing highways instead of more freeways.

<u>Reasons</u>:

The governments at all levels rush too fast to take property. Land is precious. Property ownership is sacred. The government must be forced to investigate many other creative options before taking property. As it is now, the government doesn't have to think much about taking land from the people. With this law, the final authority of eminent domain will be in the hands of the property owners, as it should be, and then the government will be forced to look at creative options.

In the early days of this country, land was plentiful. However, with the population level in this country today, and with freeways and strip malls paving the earth, there isn't much land left. The law regarding eminent domain must now be revised.

The government, at any level, cannot be as cavalier about this issue of eminent domain as they have been for so many years. All levels of government must think more carefully and be more creative.

26. <u>Eminent Domain laws must mandate that property can only be taken if the property owner agrees, or if the people approve of it in a direct vote on a November ballot.</u>

The government must prove to each property owner that the government has looked at all other options, and that taking this land is in the best interest of the public. The property owner can look at the evidence, and disagree. The property owner can suggest other alternatives. Eminent domain cannot be taken.

If after much discussion between property owner and government there is a deadlock on the issue, then it is taken up with the people. The property owners have a right to take their issue directly to the people over a period of months, with proposed alternate solutions. This is taken up for a direct vote on a regular November ballot. (No special elections at odd times).

If the people of the community vote that taking the property is in the best interest of the community, then, and only then, can eminent domain be put into effect. If, however, the people vote no, then the issue is dropped. The government cannot try to take the same property again for 10 years.

When the people approve of a property taken for eminent domain, then property owners will be compensated at top dollar for their property.

This must hold for all levels of government: city, county, state, and federal. For each area, the same rules should apply as above.

Reasons:

The governments at all levels rush too fast to take property. Land is precious. Property ownership is sacred. People work very hard much of their lives to get some property they can enjoy. As it is now, the government doesn't have to think much about taking land from the people. With the final authority in the hands of the property owners, as it should be, then people will be able to keep the property they worked so hard and so long to acquire.

Furthermore, The government will be forced to look at more creative options. If the government can't take land until the owner approves, or until the people themselves vote on it directly, then the people will double check as to whether there is a need at all for this item, and whether there isn't a better way (such as using vacant business sites or high speed rail)

In the early days of this country, land was plentiful. Therefore, no one had to think about consulting the people. There was land elsewhere for the displaced property owners to go, and so the law did not have to be revised.

However, times have changed. With the population level in this country today, and with freeways and strip malls paving the earth, there isn't much land left. The law regarding eminent domain must now be revised.

Note that the direct vote must be in November. Too many slick politicians hold elections at odd times, thereby confusing the people. This is just fraudulent voting procedures, and any laws passed this way are fraudulent.

Some may consider this discussion and voting a time consuming process. Yet think what is at stake. Once the land is gone, it is gone forever. Once the trees and grass are gone, they are gone forever. Once a person is kicked out of his home, he loses it forever. There is nothing more permanent in our country than taking property through eminent domain, except for the death penalty. We must be very deliberate, and must very careful, before taking any piece of property.

The government, at any level, cannot be as cavalier about this issue of eminent domain as they have been for so many years. All levels of government must think more carefully and be more creative.

G. <u>Privacy</u>

27. <u>The government is not allowed to sell personal information</u>

<u>Reason:</u>

Currently, governments sell personal information to businesses and organizations. This is wrong. If the department needs that information about an individual in order to run the public business, then that is fine. However, there is no reason to sell this information to others.

28. <u>Only those with authority may have access to information</u>

For example: only those in the medical profession or insurance industry can look at your medical records. Example #2: Only those in real estate, such as those selling or renting to others, have the right to see rental history. Anyone who does not have specific authority in any specific area will not be allowed to see the information. The law that is written must specifically address each area of private records, and specifically state those with authority to view information.

<u>Reason:</u>

Privacy is sacred. However, as it currently exists, there are many records which are public. There is no need for this.

There is no need for strangers to know your medical history. There is no need for strangers to know where you have lived for the past 15 years. It is very creepy to know that anyone out there can get this information on you. This must be stopped.

There are legitimate reasons for some people to know this information. For example, a businessman realtor who rents property would like to know the rental history of a potential renter. The businessman wants to be sure that he will get paid each month, and that there will be no destruction of property. Thus, he has good reason to know the rental and property ownership history of any potential customer.

However, using that same example, there is no need for strangers or criminals to know this. There are evil people everywhere, and they can use this information against you in some way. It is possible for bad people to go to those old addresses, and start asking questions about you. We must not let them have the option of invading our privacy.

29. Privacy as a Constitutional Amendment

Privacy is a fundamental right. If the founders knew what has been going on today, they would have stated this in the Bill of Rights. We must rectify this problem by putting Amendments to the Constitutions—state constitutions, and the US Constitution—guaranteeing the right to privacy.

Reason:

The right to privacy is a fundamental right. Every individual has the right to live his life as he wants, so long as it does not harm another. Furthermore, every man has the right to his private property, and what he does in his own property is his own business.

However, too often the right to privacy is being trampled on today. This comes from the government, from business, and from unscrupulous individuals.

Do note, however, that the right to privacy is limited in this regard: abuse of another. If one person forces another, or if one person steals from another, then that is a violation of that second person's rights, and therefore right to privacy does not apply. However, at the same time, if the second person consents to all the activities, and it is done in the private home, then there is no crime, and the right to privacy holds strong.

We must state this as a specific right. When we do, then our right to privacy will be much more secure.

30. Census reform—no questions on race, income, work, or home

All questions on Census regarding race, income, where you work, and personal information about your home must be stated as illegal.

Reason:

There are good items on the Census, and bad items.

The purpose of the census is for one thing only: Population. The primary purpose is for population changes, and then redistricting of the areas which representatives actually represent.

Also, there are other related, positive uses. Having full names are good for tracing family history. Knowing ages is good because it helps the city decide things such as how many schools to build. Asking questions about transportation are good because it can help the city decide what public transportation may be needed (types, and where to run it). So there are some good items on the ten year census beyond population count only.

However, there are intrusive questions. Asking about race is wrong, for we are all Americans. Asking about income is nobody's business (even so, the IRS has that information). Asking where you work or what you do is also no one's business. Asking about your home has nothing to do with the census at all.

All these intrusive questions must be stated as illegal.

31. <u>We must write laws stating very specifically where the boundaries of privacy are for business and governments, on many specific issues.</u>

<u>Reason:</u>

Businesses, governments, and bad individuals will always try to invade our privacy. They do what they can get away with. It is only if we state specific laws against these acts will these specific invasions of our privacy be stopped permanently.

I cannot list all the issues, for there are many. Here are but a few examples. Example #1: Companies that use websites track your visits, and even share that information with others. This must be stopped. Example #2: Cameras. Placement of recording devices, and the use of these devices, can be an invasion of privacy. We must state specifically where these can be used, when, and for what purposes.

0-595-31038-9

www.ingramcontent.com/pod-product-compliance
Lightning Source LLC
Chambersburg PA
CBHW061341280526
45784CB00001B/86